Overcoming Obstacles

OrangeBooks Publication

Smriti Nagar, Bhilai, Chhattisgarh - 490020

Website: **www.orangebooks.in**

First Edition, 2021

ISBN: 978-93-92878-02-2

Printed in India

OVERCOMING OBSTACLES

JIBBY PETER DCRUZ

OrangeBooks Publication

www.orangebooks.in

Only two things are important in this world.

Things that you did.

And things that you didn't.

ACKNOWLEDGMENT

Writing a book is not easy. I like to run. But I do not want to write. While running, all I need to do is keep moving forward and there is no need to retrace my steps. I wish writing were like that. I hope I did not have to frame and reframe sentences over and over again. Spending hour after hour seated on a chair and putting words together requires a particular type of stamina. It becomes even more complicated when a child runs around the house who keeps asking, "Appa, will you play with me?"

It took two years to finish this book and I could not have done it without a gentle push.

I have to start with Anooja Joseph, my wife. Everything outlined in the book was possible only because she kept supporting me all along. She is the rock upon which this book was built.

A father-daughter relationship is one of the most cherished things on earth. Everything I did and continue to do is so that Nova can someday understand the underlying purpose of what I was trying to get out of life. In the animated movie Ramayana, Hanuman lifts an entire mountain to bring the medicinal herbs growing on it to the wounded Lakshmana. Once when Nova and I watched it together, she asked me, "Appa, can you lift a mountain too?" If a 4-year-old can see the strength in you, then why can we not see it ourselves? I will wait for the day she grows up and can hear the book's contents from myself.

How can I go without mentioning my parents, Peter Simon D'cruz and Jean Peter? It is typical for a parent to be worried when their child starts running marathons with a bad leg. I can understand their concern but the need to convince them that I could still do it was even more significant. Today, they are my most incredible supporters. I also want to thank my younger brother James Peter D'cruz for making my fundraisers look good enough for social media.

A tonne of gratitude to my friend Machu Shanavas who lives 2000 km away. Machu stepped in and took the time to come out with the catchy cover page design for the book.

Though my wife had been suggesting that I put my experience into words, my student Avinash Avirachan delivered the final nudge and convinced me to make it into a book. We all need that one person who is not family to help us think big.

I take this opportunity to give a very warm hug to Leo Akash Raj, the backbone and front bone of the NGO Pretty Lil Hearts. Only because Leo interviewed me for the youtube channel 'Kanavu Katchers', I gained the courage to stand before a camera ever since. I thank him for all the activities I have done on Facebook Live and for the radio interview that came later.

Lincy John, an English professor and friend, took the time to go through the critical areas of the book and make it better. I thank her for that.

The poem 'Angels & Devils' was the first original piece of writing I ever did. I thank my two friends who motivated me to express my thoughts on a piece of paper.

Hans Zimmer is the composer of the soundtrack to the movie 'The Last Samurai.' It was only from listening to his music that I could go to a place of intense concentration and come up with the last few chapters.

There is no benefit to anyone if I overcame obstacles and kept the newly attained energy just for myself. We have been put here on earth to keep the river of inspiration flowing and pass it onto the next person. I want to express my deep gratitude to all the ambitious runners, cyclists and swimmers in the 'Team Learners' WhatsApp group. They would give me a thumbs-up whenever I set out to do something.

And I am not quite sure if the final acknowledgment should go to 'God' or 'The Universe' or 'The Great Spirit' out there. Whatever it is, I cannot thank you enough for sharing a part of your energy to move through life.

CONTENTS

WHAT WILL OTHERS THINK?

"അവർ എന്നെ കളിയാക്കുമോ?" (Will they make fun of me?)

That is what my 4-year-old daughter said when I asked her if she was ready to come to my gym and do some push-ups there. If a small child is affected by what others think, imagine how much we let others limit us every day.

Most people make life-changing decisions all the time. But those decisions get destroyed by listening to the opinion of others. People are most happy whenever they see you doing what they have been comfortably doing all their lives. But you are not them, are you? If you can realize that you were born to be unique, soon you will start to create a path of your own.

And what you think about you equally matters as well. Just because you were introverted or depressed or neurotic in the past does not mean that you have to stick that label onto your forehead forever. Behaviour modification is entirely possible. New exposures and the right people can do wonders in your life.

Since childhood, we have conditioned ourselves to stay away from the rain. The rain is not the problem. What the rain represents is the problem. All we hear are the voices of our 'loved ones' who brainwashed us with their broken view of life whenever it rains.

Do not listen to that voice.

Follow the latest trend and you too will be a follower. That will only make you invisible.

If you want to be different, then stand out from the rest. True strength comes from being unique.

I am an ultramarathoner and ultra conscious in buying ultra-healthy foods. I often get the question, "Aren't fruits, nuts and seeds expensive?"

Everyone wants to compare expensive foods against cheap foods. That is where the ignorant need to change the way they think. I do not waste money going to the movies, buying new clothes during festivities, and on the latest gadgets, vacations, or alcohol. I choose not to waste money on material aspects that do not make me better. Things and possessions do not enrich you. Experiences do.

So get back to doing what you loved doing. Then that becomes your only world.

Any mistakes made by children on paper are easily erasable when they use pencils. When they turned into adults, pens replaced pencils. Every mistake remained permanently on their page. Similarly, most adults will look back on every mistake and let life stop them from trying new things.

Be like a kid.

There was a girl in my school who said, "Jibby, you are a fool. You will believe anything you hear."

Eighteen years since then, I'm still a fool.

I'm a fool for hearing my inner voice say, "You can climb Malayatoor hill ten times in one day."

I'm a fool for hearing my inner voice say, "You can run a marathon in the summer in the sun and raise money for charity."

I'm a fool for hearing my inner voice say, "You can run 4 miles every 4 hrs for 48 hours."

I'm a fool for hearing my inner voice say, "You can do 1000 push-ups in 100 mins."

I'm a fool for hearing my inner voice say, "You can do fundraisers for the needy on your own."

I like being a fool.

Just follow your heart and do not listen to anyone outside it.

There was a guy who encouraged me when I started running. He would ride up to me as I ran and pat me on the back as I was training for a 4 km race. A few years later, when I told him that I was doing a 300 km ride for charity, he did not motivate me. He advised me that I have a family. He informed me that I had a limit. And he advised me not to make cycling a craze.

It is funny that whenever you start on something, people will congratulate you and motivate you. But when you become genuinely dedicated and obsessed about it, they call you crazy and do their best to discourage you.

Why is that?

Because they cannot imagine themselves ever doing it, there are many forces in this world trying to put limits on our minds and body. All the inventions and achievements you came to know are by people who did not believe in limits.

So the next time someone calls you crazy, tell them, "Sorry, I'm not crazy. I'm just not like you." Running 4 miles every 4 hrs for 48 hrs will toughen your mind to deal with life. But all people see is that you are insane. They will never know the mental strength one acquires from doing such things. It is ok, and they do not need to know. You do not need to explain. When you do things that are crazy-hard like that, sooner or later, people will notice a change in your character.

I have had comments to keep my endurance activities as an occasional passion but not turn it into an addiction.

And I would reply "കൊച്ചു പിള്ളേരെ നോക്കുന്നത് ഒരു അമ്മയുടെ വല്ലപ്പോഴും ഉള്ള പാഷൻ ആണോ അതോ

അഡിക്ഷൻ ആണോ?"

(For a mother, is looking after a child an occasional passion or an addiction?)

It is because mothers are addicted to their children that the child develops wonderfully. So do not waste any more time thinking about what others will think of you.

"Get busy living or get busy dying."

(From the movie 'The Shawshank Redemption')

BABY STEPS, ALL OVER AGAIN

Being my younger brother's first day of school in the 11th grade, he wanted to make quite an impression before his classmates at SNV Sanskrit Higher Secondary School. One way of doing it is to have his brother, clad in black tees and black jeans, pick him up after school on a very noisy and very hip Suzuki Samurai. It was my cousin's bike. So there I was on a Saturday afternoon leaving home sporting the 'bad boy' look. It was also the last time I would leave home with my left Anterior Cruciate Ligament (ACL) entirely intact.

Halfway to the destination, I found myself behind a 20-foot truck. I'm not particularly eager to drive fast, but I cannot tolerate riding behind slow-moving trucks. There were only two lanes on the road, one to go forward and the other for oncoming traffic. After spending a minute or two trying to overtake the damn vehicle, I had the weirdestimage of me crashing my bike.

> *"If something can go wrong, it will."*
>
> - Murphy's Law

When the opportunity to overtake came up, I went for it. Little did I know that my cousin had powered down the bike to get more mileage out of it. Little did I also know that the trucker was about to overtake another vehicle in front of it. As I was halfway there, the truck steered to its side, totally unaware of my presence. I braked just in time, but the rear end of the vehicle tapped my shoulder.

I fell off the bike onto my left side. Because I had a helmet on, my skull was intact. Onlookers rushed to pick me up. Falling on my left rib put me out of breath. There was also numbness in my left knee, but I still tried to stand on it.

Big mistake!

The anterior cruciate ligament (ACL) is one of the key ligaments that stabilize the knee joint. It connects the thigh bone with the shinbone. Any impact over it will most likely tear the ligament.

My left knee popped out of its socket.

That made me lift my leg. In doing so, it popped back in by itself. I tried to stand on it again. It got dislocated and relocated again. That was when I knew I was screwed. I was hanging onto an onlooker's shoulder when the driver of the truck ran towards me. Not pointing fingers, I put the entire blame on myself and got into a taxi rickshaw to the nearby hospital with my leg sticking out at the side.

I arrived at the Casualty Department of a nearby hospital with only twenty rupees in my pocket. After paying for the ride, now there was none. As I was moving in a wheelchair, I phoned Issac. Issac is that person in the family whom my brother and I contact whenever we mess up things. A nurse helped me up onto a bed. This bed was the same one my brother James used a year ago when he arrived here with a broken arm from a bicycle stunt gone wrong.

"Crap! He is going to have a lot of fun poking on my wounds," I told myself because that was what I did back then. You only get what you give. That is karma.

"Are you wearing underwear?"

That question from the nurse interrupted my thought. She wanted me to remove my pants.

"We need to have a look at that knee." she continued. Meanwhile, my brother was still waiting at the school front. After half an hour, he took the bus home.

Back at the hospital, the general physician suspected I had a torn ligament. But since it was Saturday evening, the specialist was off-duty and would be back only by Monday. That meant I would have to spend the whole of Sunday doing nothing in the hospital. When Issac finally arrived, he convinced me to move to another hospital. Fortunately, the duty doctor was present. After I took the X-ray, he confirmed that the ACL suffered a minor tear. Blood had also accumulated inside my knee from the rupture. At the time, any upper body movement was excruciating on the ribs as it had absorbed most of the impact during the fall. Getting onto the stretcher from the wheelchair was one of the most severe pain I had ever experienced. With one gentle stab, the nurse pushed an enormous needle into the knee joint. She changed syringes until the nurse drew out all of the extra blood. I was sent home after the procedure with a cast that

prevented the knee from bending. I also had several patches on my shoulder, arms and palms. Brother counted 17 injuries when I got home.

As I fell asleep that night, I recalled the doctor's words. He said, "Jibby, an ACL tear will never fully heal. The best you can expect is an 80% recovery." He also advised me to take complete rest for a month.

"Will I ever be able to use my legs as I used to?" I was worried.

The next day I woke up in pain. Ants had found their way to the dressing on my shoulder, and these were the biting type. Going to the toilet with an unbendable leg was the most fun. To move around in the house, I had to use a four-legged walker.

On the third day, I had my first gas attack. It was in the chest and abdomen. It went away in a couple of minutes, but even moving a muscle caused extreme pain during that time. Somehow the accident never really upset me after the initial shock. I tried not to get lost in thought about what would happen. One way I did that was by spending a majority of my waking hours reading books. I read through 'The Autobiography of Malcolm X' and 'Growing Up

Bin Laden' in just a week.

Since I had scratched the outsides of my palm from the accident, I could not bend or wet them for two weeks. Mother had to spoon-feed me. A neighbour by the name of Rachel made daily visits to clean my wounds with antiseptic ointments.

It was not a fun feeling.

In two weeks, I was able to transition from the walker to a walking stick. After a month, it was time to have the cast removed, and I could not prepare for what came next.

My left thigh had shrunk to half of what it used to be. It was a real eye-opener. The doctor told me that the muscle loss was due to a lack of movement in that area. He assured me that it would get back to its original size through proper physiotherapy and strengthening exercises.

No matter what I have tried, my left muscle remains slightly smaller than my right.

"Lift your leg." the doctor told me. I could not.

It was a strange feeling to keep signalling the leg to move but be unable to do so.

"Doctor, I can't" I replied. This experience was the most saddening and paralyzing feeling I have ever had in my life.

"You can! Lift your leg, man!" he kept repeating.

Finally, I was able to but barely. Oh, and one more thing.

Wearing the cast for a month had other impacts. I could not bend my knee.

I left the hospital utterly depressed that day. A strap-on knee immobilizer replaced the cast. I also had to continue using the walking stick for balance as my left leg was still weak. I could drive a car but not walk without assistance. How funny was that!

Getting back to work was challenging. It was the first time

everyone got to see a faculty of Viswajyothi College moving around with a walking stick. (Apart from my department head Mr. Jose P Varghese, who was affected by polio) The college has its various sections built on different elevations, which made things only harder. On an average day of work, I had to climb over one hundred steps. But then again, that is what you get for being impatient on the bike.

This is my doing. I brought this on myself. There is really no one else to blame.

After a month of walking around like this, I was strong enough to walk unassisted. But I had to be extremely careful. There were times when I would be walking through hallways and would lose balance. It was because I had been walking close to the wall that I did not fall over. Soon I got rid of the knee-immobilizer too. The doctor advised me to sit at the edge of the table and apply downward pressure on my left knee to get my knee moving again. Every bit of motion gained by the knee was achieved at the cost of immense pain.

Months before the accident, my family had booked tickets to spend a week in Delhi and the pink city of Rajasthan. Now two months into the accident, the Onam holidays were fast approaching. Bad knee or not, my parents decided the family trip would take place as scheduled. It was because they wanted me to spend time outside the house and get my legs moving again, without the strap-on and the walking stick.

We got to Delhi by train and made the return journey by flight. Most of the historical places we visited on the first day had slight elevation. My family spent the second-day visiting old forts and palaces in and around Delhi. These had considerable heights. Making my way up to forts on hilltops was a daunting task. But I did have my brother's shoulder to lean onto at all times. By nightfall, my knee hurt so much that I could feel a grinding sensation inside it. It was comforting to find a hotel bed and crash into it.

Amer Fort at Jaipur

The next place to visit was Jaipur which had more forts. All of them had a great view from the top, but it felt as though I had to earn every one of those beautiful sights with my bad leg. At Amer Fort, I had the rare opportunity to get a cobra wrapped around my neck from a snake-charmer.

Eventually, I did get my knee to bend as much as it did. Over a few months, I gained back most of the quad muscles. I am technically not supposed to do marathons or ultra-marathons, let alone go for morning jogs with such a medical history. I am not supposed to go for 10,000 feet hikes too.

But I did.

Never let anyone or anything tell you what you are supposed to or not supposed to do. Adversities are blessings in disguise. I guarantee you that these adversities will not feel like a blessing while you are going through them. The 'blessing' part comes after you push through it.

Six years after the fortunate accident, I got into endurance running. It was not because I could run that I got into running.

I started running because I could not.

CHASING NOVA

In Latin, the word Nova means 'new'. In astronomy, it means a newborn star that shines a thousand times brighter than how it later will be. Among the Native American names for girl-child, it means 'butterfly chaser.' Nova is also the name of my lovely daughter. But before I would get the naming rights for my baby girl, let me first tell you how all that came to be.

My wife and I decided that a year after we tied the knot would be the right time to go for a baby. The first time she got pregnant, it was beautiful. We went through all the emotions any typical parent-to-be would go through. At the time, she had to make a round trip of 120 km to her workplace daily. She did this until the first trimester and then got employed at a place near home. The ultrasound scan at three months showed a very healthy baby. Soon the scanning for the fifth month was due. Usually, five months into the pregnancy period, all of the baby's organs would have formed. My wife and I were at the hospital. The procedure was to get the scanning done by the ultrasound specialist and then have it analyzed by the consulting doctor. This time my wife wanted to see the live video of the baby during the scan. I waited outside the ultrasound room with a book to keep me company.

Coming out of the scanning room, I remember her looking very concerned.

Wiping the tears off her face, she said, "The scanning doctor did not show me the video of the baby through the monitor. He told me that the consulting doctor would explain everything."

I did not get up from my seat. I did not even let go of the book from my hand. I knew this was not going to end well. But at that moment, I chose to be the stronger one and said, "Let us wait and hear what the doctor has to say." She went back inside the waiting room, which other women fully occupied. Each time the nurse came out of the consulting doctor's room to call patients, I could see through the glass door my disheartened wife's face turning in that direction. Finally, the nurse called her name, and we went in.

After going through the scanning report, the doctor broke the news that the baby's kidneys are grossly disfigured. There was not much amniotic fluid inside the uterus due to a blockage in the urethra of the fetus. It was causing the urine to go back to the kidneys, thereby damaging them

beyond repair. My wife was devastated. Immediately she burst into tears. We got a second opinion from another hospital, and the reports proved the same.

With a heavy heart, we decided to abort the baby.

The doctor would administer a drug that would stop the baby's heartbeat and induce natural delivery. I even remember asking the pediatrician, "What if the drug does not work and the baby is still alive when the delivery takes place?"

Fortunately, that did not happen.

A month later, my wife got back to her work as an assistant professor. Soon after, she got pregnant again. The doctor advised bed rest. So she had to take a leave of absence from work. But that did not do any good. Two months into the pregnancy, for reasons unknown, she had minor bleeding in the uterus. I remember getting the call about it at my workplace. My family took her to the hospital. When I reached the hospital, I found out that the fetus had no heartbeat. My wife was already in the operation theatre. Once again, the doctors removed the dead fetus as before.

My wife was going through an emotional holocaust. I wish I could explain the mindset my wife was in, but I really cannot. It was not me who had to get into the labour room once again. It was not me who had to go through the whole process again. It was not me who had to deliver a dead baby twice. So I am not qualified to comment on that. But after two failed pregnancies, I was beginning to prepare myself for the possibility that I may never become a father.

Fortunately, that did not happen.

Now, we were more determined than ever to have a baby.

In 2016, she got pregnant for the third time. This time we had a change of doctor. Taking into consideration Anooja's medical history, she needed complete bed rest. Under no circumstance was she to get out of bed unless to take a bath or use the loo.

We made it to the baby shower in the ninth month. I even bought a stethoscope to hear the baby's heartbeat. Since the stethoscope was a cheap one, we could not listen to it. So I bought a Doppler heartbeat sensor with a built-in loudspeaker. Only one time in the ninth month did we use it successfully. A couple of days after the baby shower, it was time to admit her into the hospital. Surprisingly, she went into labour pain the very evening she got there.

"Oh my God!" exclaimed the nurse at the labour room when she checked to see the cervical opening.

"Your water just broke," she said.

Now the contractions began to get stronger. Four hours later, at midnight of April 4th 2017, the miracle of God we had so long been waiting for was born. It was a girl. I named her Nova. Just like a star, she would henceforth bring much joy and brightness into our life. Finally, we became a family. And finally, I chased 'the butterfly chaser' and caught up with her.

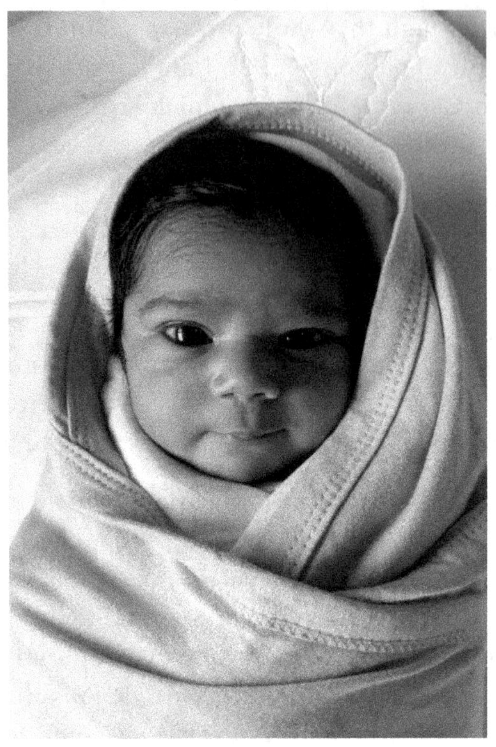

Nova at day 2

FROM BABY STEPS TO NEVER-ENDING STEPS

It had been four months since Nova was born. In September 2017, during the Onam vacation, a long-lost desire popped into my head.

"Why not give another go at that 4km race I was so miserable at?" I thought.

Six years earlier, I took part in a 4km race in my village. Trying to do it without stopping, I almost fainted at the third kilometer and had to walk the rest of the run. The next edition of the race was in December. Would three months be enough to train? Will my lousy knee hold up?

Who knows? But I sure am going to try.

So on the very next day of my running inception, I was outside wearing sandals with backstraps and ready to set to start training. But where would I run? Running on the main roads was out of the question. I did not want my villagers to have that surprised look on their faces seeing me huffing and puffing like a tired dog. Because back in 2017, going on a run was an unusual thing for a 30-year-old to do.

There was a narrow stretch of a pocket road partially lit by street lamps and 400 meters long. It was perfect for me.

Train like a ghost so that one day you may reveal yourself in the light for the whole world to see.

Running at night meant that I would not be noticed by many. Even if they did, they would not bother to ask too many questions at that time of the day. With no proper training plan, I decided to do a continuous run twice along this road. It was only 800 meters, and I was out of breath.

Was this the after-effect of the Tuberculosis Bacteria I caught four years ago? I recalled coughing my lungs out for a whole month until I got the proper treatment.

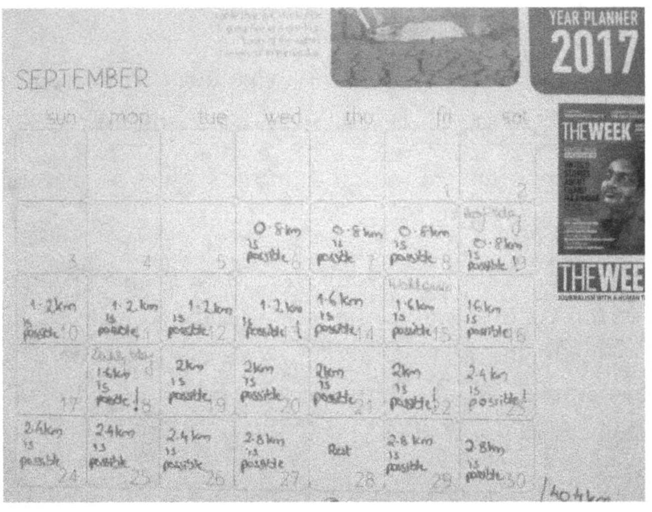

This calendar was the only thing that kept me motivated

The next night I was back at the same place and went the same distance. On the fifth day, it felt comfortable, and I ran an extra 400 meters. Now the new length was 1.2km. That was how I decided to increase the distance by 400 meters every five days.

In a month, I had achieved the seemingly impossible task of running nonstop for 4 kilometers.

Armed with the newly gained confidence and endurance, the next day, I took to the main roads of my village and successfully ran the actual racecourse. It got to the point where I was able to run 10km in a single stretch. In three months, a half marathon by the name of Spice Coast Marathon came up. When I told my parents that I would participate, they reminded me that I had a bad leg. Determined to prove them wrong, I still went ahead and completed those 21.1kms in 2 hours and 45 mins using the run-walk method. I took a moment to thank everything out there that helped me accomplish this. Plus, I got to see Sachin Tendulkar, who flagged off the event. People were more interested in getting his autograph than running the marathon.

My experiment with endurance running should have stopped after that run. I had achieved the satisfaction of running 4 km and, on top of that, completed a half marathon too.

But no, life did not let me stop there. All thanks to my wife.

A week after the marathon, I got into a quarrel with my wife for reasons I cannot recall now. It was one of those silly husband-wife fights that most 'happily married' couples must go through before they start behaving like adults. The fight got resolved within a day. But at that moment, I planned to run 16 km nonstop the next day. It was how I dealt with anger back then. Jumping from 10 km to a 16 km continuous run seemed to be the perfect solution to extinguish my anger. Of course, she was informed about this only after the run went well.

A week later, thanks to another fight, I did a continuous half marathon. It only took 2 hours and 30 mins. I had to imagine Jesus Christ and Buddha running beside me to complete the damn thing. Then a month later, I went on to do the Trivandrum Marathon (42.2 km). A year later, a 60km ultra-marathon and even more.

Just look at all the events that had to happen in my life to get me into running. Everything makes sense when you look back. It is why I never question whenever things go wrong for me. There is always something to be learned from every one of them. They are all blessings in disguise.

Everybody needs two basic things functioning well for any run. They are lungs and legs. And those that I had were not a hundred percent. In the process of training for a short race, I discovered that my legs and lungs were not as bad as I thought they were.

It is the same as running a marathon. Everything will make sense once you cross the finishing line.

42222222222.2K

A marathon remains one of the most feared events in sporting history. Getting your body to keep moving forward for 42.2kms requires a considerable commitment on your part. It takes anywhere from two hours for an elite runner to seven hours for an average runner to complete a marathon distance. No matter how many times they do it, it remains a challenge for the average runner. They want to make it across the finish line in one piece. Elite runners, on the other hand, try to run it as fast as possible. Even if you are in your best condition, numerous things can go wrong once your race starts.

Long-distance running places a highly demanding load on the legs. The body tries to direct more resources into the legs to keep it moving. If there is too much food in the stomach, that can lead to one of two problems.

You could develop an upset stomach and lose control of your bowels. Or, if you are the type that likes to go fast, there is a slim chance that your mid-race nutrition will be hard to digest. And what do you think happens to food that remains undigested in the stomach?

It gets vomited out.

Muscle cramps, heatstroke and side-stitch, are the other things that can appear out of nowhere. It says that every runner runs two-thirds of a marathon with his legs and the remaining one-third with his heart. On an empty stomach, our bodies store enough glycogen to fuel a runner for about 30 km. Beyond that, the runner has to manage the nutrition consumed during the run. And if you are making a trail (off-road) run with elevation, then all these problems move on to a different level.

After the Spice Coast Marathon of 2017, I came to know of the upcoming Vagamon Ultrail in January 2018. Trail running looked super fun. Who wouldn't love to spend long hours in a mountain region like Vagamon? The experience would surely be unforgettable. It was the perfect

opportunity to reconnect with nature at its finest. But registrations for that were already closed. Eager to meet the qualifying criteria for the 2019 edition, I registered for the Trivandrum Midnight Marathon just three days before the event. Keep in mind this was only four months after I had gotten into running. Running a full marathon did not seem scary at the time. My logic was that if I could do a half marathon in under 3 hours, then a full marathon which was twice the distance, could be done in under 6 hours.

Hehe.

The only plan was to do it. It was one of those "Look After You Leap" strategies.

The date for the marathon was December 10th at 00.00 hours. Like the previous race, my parents reminded me that I had a bad knee. After a six-hour journey by bus, I arrived at Trivandrum city to collect the pre-race kit. Finally, I made it to my accommodation at 6 pm. At 8.30 pm, I woke up after sleeping for an hour and a half.

The tension was starting to grow.

The race organizers conducted the full marathon along with the half marathon. It was going to be a loop run. The half marathoners had to make the same loop twice, while the full marathoners had to do it four times.

At midnight, the run began. All I had on me was a keypad phone, a piece of printed paper and a 250 rupee digital watch. The printed paper showed the distance I had to cover against the respective times. The cut-off time for the full marathon was 6 hours.

I completed half the distance in 2 hours and 20 minutes. Most of the half marathoners had completed their two loops. It also came to my attention that only 13 runners were doing the full marathon. Soon things would start to get more challenging than I could ever imagine. There is a saying that your first marathon feels like giving birth to a child. That's how hard it is going to be.

My legs were starting to feel heavy. My lower back, for lack of strength, was trying its best to keep my body vertical. It was at this time that another guy in his 40's caught up with me. He looked strong enough to do this. So I threw an invisible anchor around him and tried to run with him as far as I could. The man did his best to motivate me. He urged me to run continuously on all the flat portions of the road and up to the water stations. The back pain was now unbearable to handle on my own. Spraying volini replaced the pain with the feeling of a burn.

At some point in the run, I forgot to use the spray available at a water station. That shot up my back pain again, and I could no longer maintain the other runner's pace. I wished him to do his best, and he went on.

My lower back now felt paralyzed. I wanted to sit down beside the road and cool off for a few minutes. The clock was ticking and I had to prove to my parents and the world that I could finish this in time. I was running by myself in my first marathon with no one to look for hope. There was 12 km more to go.

That was when I rang up my wife at 4.15 in the morning.

"You have got to help me. I cannot do this on my own." I cried to her.

"Please stay awake and keep sending me messages until I finish this!" I said, and I hung up.

Soon she started texting me messages like: "Cmooooooooonnnnnnn Buuuuuu! You can do it!!!!!"

'Bu' is the term used by Anglo-Indian women to call their husbands affectionately. Reading her messages from 200 kms away was like a candle in the dark for me.

I also had one other trick to keep me motivated. It was a soundtrack named 'Tomorrow' from the movie 'Ali'. In the film, there is a part where Muhammed Ali, the boxer, goes on a training run before his big fight with George Foreman. 'Tomorrow' is the song that plays in the background. It is one of the high points in the movie. With this song on repeat, I ran the remaining distance as hard and as long as possible.

I could feel something was not right inside my shoes. Some of my toes felt funny. But there was not enough time to remove them and see what had happened. Every minute was precious.

Imagine having your innocent soul juiced in a blender, and you have to drink it without stopping for a breath.

That was how it felt that night.

"I am going to finish this even if it kills me!" I said to a volunteer as I approached a water station at kilometer 34.

In times of hardship, it is of the utmost importance what you say to yourself. Others may not believe in you. The whole world may not believe in you. Even if all hope seems lost, there is still hope in you.

And that is all that matters.

The end was now in sight. But the time was almost up. With one last push, I made a sprint to the finishing line.

The race officials could not confirm if I had made it in under 6 hours or not. I would have to wait for the timing results from the electronic chip to be processed. They told me that I would receive the results on my phone.

By now, it did not matter if I had made the cut-off or not. What mattered was that I had given my absolute best in this run. After a long bus ride on the same day with very little nutrition and very

little sleep, completing a marathon was good enough for me. I phoned my family and informed them of the good news. My wife was ecstatic.

"I am so proud of you." said my father.

My department head at the workplace, Jose P Varghese, also congratulated me.

In two hours, I was on my way back home. That was when I received the timing result.

"Congratulations Jibby Peter D'cruz. You have completed the 2017 Trivandrum Midnight Marathon in 05:59:08."

STEPPING STAIRS TO SUCCESS

Dear Darling-Daughter Nova,

Let this hopefully be the first of my everlasting gifts to you. A gift of memory. A gift that may rejuvenate you whenever you are in search of that elusive inner strength.

After a whole year, the wait was finally over. It was a joyous moment for your mother and me to watch your first fumbling steps. A couple of weeks later, you were walking just as well as any other toddler could. Two more months went by, and we were eager to see you do more. So there we were as a family at the ground floor of India's largest shopping mall, Lulu Mall. You were up in my arms, taking in all the unfamiliar sights of the mall. It was then that a thought crossed my mind.

"Why not see if you could make it to the top floor?"

Lulu mall had four floors. After getting the green light from the wife, I decided to put this to the test.

"Nova, shall we use the steps?" You broke into a smile.

With your little palm wrapped around my finger, you were making the climb one step at a time. Other people and their children waiting for the escalator looked in awe as we happily moved up. Throughout the time, you were never out of breath. Soon all three of us were on the top floor of the mall. Your mother captured a photograph to cherish the moment.

Sure, parents may think this would not be an appropriate thing for a child as young as you. But they do not understand that we only wanted to sow the seeds of strength and perseverance into you early. Let this be an unforgettable memory for you. Use this whenever you doubt your power. I am sure every daughter wants to be reassured by her parents that she is beautiful. Yes Nova, you are and will always stay that way. But more than beauty, we want you to be bold.

More than being cute, we want you to be charismatic. Recalling this feat will serve as a spark to ignite your efforts to accomplish bigger and better feats in life.

It is not a big thing. Nor is it a small thing. But it certainly is something.

On reaching the top floor

*"If you want your daughter to be courageous,
don't tell her she is beautiful; instead, tell her she is courageous"*

FUELING LIFE

A runner's point-of-view of the events that happened during the 2019 Vagamon Ultrail 60K so wonderfully organized by Soles of Cochin.

With the wind waving at my face,

With the glance of green glittering in my eyes,

With the setting sun stroking the orange sky,

I see satisfaction in swinging branches.

I see restlessness in the rustling leaves.

I see silence in still waters.

Though a newbie into running, I can affirm that there is no mountain high enough to dampen a person's soul. The 5th of January 2019 will stand as a witness for all of time to those who ran their legs and their hearts out. One thing about racing is that it hurts. You better accept that from the beginning, or you are not going to get anywhere.

The real purpose of running is not to win a race. It is to test the limits of the human heart.

Waking up at 4.30 am after an anxious and sleepless night, I remember the morning of race day being a very starry one. You could almost draw the course map of Vagamon Ultrail by connecting those stars that were so close to each other. It was another add-on of not doing a city-run. And what a chilly morning it was! Enrolled into the 60K category, I offered a moment of prayer to all the 90K category runners who started at 5 am. It was a time long before they got to see the sun or feel any warmth whatsoever. But this is running, so it is alright. Being my first-ever ultra and with no knowledge of the outcome, I declined the organizers' pre-race peanut butter and jam sandwiches. With a very enthusiastic countdown at 6.30 in the morning, the 2019 Vagamon Ultrail 60K was off! It was encouraging to see everyone set off into the unknown. And looking back now from the comfort of my home, what an adventure it was.

The trail began almost immediately. Half an hour into the run, I got lost and was not even aware of it. Luckily, the very experienced and previous year's best-timer in the 50K general women's category Mahalakshmi the Missile, was quick to spot the absence of those trail-marker ribbons.

"Memories are the fuel to life. Make sure you create enough memories to last a lifetime."

Five hundred metres of backtracking did not do much damage, and we were back on course. Unlike a road trip, everything slows down in time when you are running. I felt the land beneath my feet, the twists, and turns of the tea-estates. The ups and downs of the course were comparable with the ups and downs in my life. The high-rising pine trees gave me high hopes. It was easy running so far. Well, that was all about to change after two idlis and sambar from the first rest area at Ammachi's House at kilometer 24

90K category runner Laura Kline tearing through Pine Forest Photo Courtesy: Vibin Balakrishnan, Thrissur

That monstrous hill, we all cursed, nearly broke me. If you thought the upward climb was tiring, I lack words to describe the way down. 'Pain-fest,' I guess. Painful on the quads. Painful on the toenails. I started hearing comments like "I do not like this" from fellow runners. Traversing the Malayatoor hill a few weeks before the race did help me to a small extent in dealing with this.

> *"Anything other than survival requires a little effort."*

A few kilometers down the hill, this creation of God disguised as father and son supplying drinking water to the runners from a bucket. If only it were possible to show those blessed souls our gratitude today. Then came the 'egg station'. It was an aid station where the very spirited race volunteers served us much-needed love. The love assumed the form of a shaken, not stirred ginger-mint-lime-and-what-not-mystery drink with hot omelets. If there ever was heaven on earth, it was at that egg station on that particular day. Speaking on everyone's behalf, I think it brought back energy and vigor into the run. What an ultra-marathon does, among other things, is that it bridges countries together. Now I have friends in Oman too. (Isn't that right, Mr. Viju the Wanderer?) Viju had come from Oman for this. We all wandered into Vagamon, seeking that vital component missing in our lives, and got so much more in the process.

The second rest area at MMJ House at kilometer 43 gave me comfort and relief. On one side, sweet potatoes were steaming. That was how I had them for the very first time. On the other side, runners were getting their legs stretched. After the aid station at Tree Stub Junction, I reached the 50 km mark. One big scoop of mixed dry fruits fueled the remaining 10 km. From there on, the rest of the course was run-able. And it was the most satisfying feeling. I had been saving my phone battery for the last leg of the run. Mp3 switched on, and I was running on nitrous all the way. Power walked all the ups. By now, I was sure that the run could be completed on time. Amid all that pain, I gave thanks to the Almighty. Recalling everything it took me to get here, tears of bliss followed. Tears are good. They are painkillers. Now my roomie, Mohan the Magnificent, and I were constantly catching up with each other throughout the run. Somewhere in between, he sped past me, and I lost sight of him. Trying to catch up with him was the most exciting run I got to do. That never happened, though. But it's alright.

"Don't run to add days to your life. Run to add life to your days."

"Just a kilometer left," cheered on by a volunteer. That was music to my ears. It was surprising to find a volunteer from Soles of Cochin to run along the last part of the race. For the first time in my life, everything was silent. All I could hear was, "200 meters only! C'mon! 100 meters more!" And there it was! The finish line. People I did not know and whom I had never met were cheering for me to cross it.

"The thrill of the hunt is in the chase, not in the catch."

After running 11 hours, 2 minutes and 51 seconds through every kind of terrain possible, finally I got my few seconds of pure happiness. I also recalled the day I had that bike accident. Today I can firmly say that there are no terrible incidents in life. There is only cause and effect. If that accident had not happened,

"Running is hard. The hard is what makes it great."

"If it doesn't challenge you, then it won't change you."

I would have never picked up running. Only at the limit of impossibility will you discover what is truly possible. On the other end of suffering, you will find great things unlike any other.

1kM^2

Waking up and using those few seconds to get a grip on the world, I knew what I had to do that day. With all the nutrition and supplies loaded into the car, I reached the base of Malayattoor hill before dawn. After a prayer in Sanskrit and the headlamp turned on, I started the day's run at 6 am. And it would not end until a self-imposed goal of completing a 42.2K marathon followed by a full trek of the Malayatoor hill was done.

At least, that was the goal. The run was to be done on the 7km road that stretched between Malayattoor and Mulamkuzhy (Illithodu) with an elevation gain of 115 meters. And for the marathon, I would have to run along that route six times which amounts to an added elevation gain of 690 metres. And if that was not enough, the extra hill to climb had an elevation of 325m. The entire ascent totalled a little over 1000 meters. That is what the 1kM2 means. The 'k' stood for a kilometre of elevation gain from the marathon and Malayattoor hill. 'M2' meant the marathon and Malayattoor.

Trying not to be weighed down by the burden of the task, I resumed running on that moonless night. Early morning runs give the day a fresh start. All that unused energy in the air when everyone else is asleep is right there for you to tap into. Everything is super quiet. There is just you, your footsteps, and your breath, all three trying to make sense of each other.

"What do you get from running this far?" somebody once asked me.

There is a technique for not going out of breath. Focus on keeping the heart rate low. Be intelligent enough not to exert too much. Take it slow. Be here and now. As I was paying attention to all these, out of nowhere, a dog sped past just inches of me. It nearly gave me a heart attack. After fending off the animal with my headlamp, I resumed running. The sub-goal was to run non-stop the first four sets of the 7km road followed by a short rest whenever a 7km distance was done.

"Why spend 2000 rupees to take part in ultra-marathons?" I was asked once.

Forty-five minutes into the task, and the Mahogany Thottam Forest check-post gate was in sight. With a gentle touch on it, that part of the run came to a stop, and I took a break for refreshment. I had cashew nuts and raisins. The return non-stop runs back to Malayatoor was done comfortably too. The third and fourth 7 km were completed with much difficulty. 28 km were done, and only 14 km more to go for the full marathon part.

With oranges in my mouth during a rest period, I noticed a candle-selling lady looking at me. Why not share some? There were 5 of those ladies. After having a brief conversation with them, I now knew how to repay the universe if I were to complete the day's task. More on that later.

The sun was now directly above my head. C'mon! I had to make just one more loop, and the running part would be done. This time I did not have the strength to run uphills. It happens if you do not spend enough time strengthening your lower back. As a result, I had to drag myself along those uphills. It was such a relief to find a local water pipe and cool myself off. After touching the check post at Mahogany Thottam for the third and final time, 35km was done. A flick of the finger on the gate reminded me that I had 7km more to go. It was at this time that I noticed two lovers in their teens talking to each other. They were holding hands at the park beside the check post. Holding hands must have felt good. 'Feeling good' was a feeling I had not been having for the past 7 hours. A woman and her husband generously offered me some water from their home. They must have surely seen the 'good feeling' on my face in this sunny weather.

"Bless them", I thought.

The man of the house, Mr. Devassy, enquired if I was doing this as a training run. They had been noticing me since six in the morning. He asked me about my job and my hometown as I drank two glasses of water and a glass of lime water from the shop he was running. I thanked them for the generosity they offered and did my last leg of the run. The marathon part was done by 2 pm. That meant 690m of elevation gain. Thank God.

"Why is he running at noon?" somebody once asked my wife.

With Malayatoor hill looking down on me, my quest to do something unique was far from over. There was no question of me not being able to climb it. But could I do the climb without stopping? That was the real challenge. Are my legs strong enough to do so after a full marathon?

After 35 minutes of huffing and puffing, I reached the top but was flat face-first on the ground soon after. Deep in my heart, I knew what it took to get to the top. Hard work, suffering, and injuries on the way were the other mountains that needed climbing too. Everything pays off in the end. And finally, at 3.30 in the afternoon, as my feet took their final steps off the hill, I had done it. Running with an ascent of 690 meters and 325 meters of a technical hill added a good 1015 meters of elevation gain.

"Why did he spend 1500 rupees on candles that he doesn't need?" nobody asked me.

Giving back matters. Yes, I did something different that day. But I was not alone. There was always some unseen and unbounded force that kept pushing me. So, it is only fair that I returned a tiny portion of the energy I was blessed with. And I did it by purchasing candles from those lovely ladies at Malayattoor. Ten candle-selling ladies must have gone home a tiny bit happier that day. It meant a lot.

All the candles bought for Rs.1500 One more story to tell Nova when she grows up.

MALAYATTOOR TOP TEN

Malayattoor is a village in Kerala. The name 'Malayattoor' is a combination of three words. Mala (Mountain), Arr (River) and Oore (Place). That is, Malayattoor is a meeting place of mountains, rivers, and land. There is a church situated atop Malayatoor Hill. The church is dedicated to St. Thomas, the apostle of Jesus Christ. St. Thomas is believed to have prayed at this shrine. On his way to Mylapore, St. Thomas stopped at Malayattoor, where he was not welcomed happily and had to run for his life to the hilltop. According to local legends, when St. Thomas prayed to the Lord and touched the rock, blood sprang forth. This made the Malayattoor Hill one of Kerala's most influential Christian pilgrim centers and attracted devotees from Kerala and the neighboring states.

But that was not what attracted me.

From base to the top, it rises 325 metres in height at a distance of 1.7 km. The terrain is also a class 2 technical type (where one may need to use hands occasionally to navigate). That is because the route is laden with boulders of all sizes. But it also has a reasonable amount of tree cover.

After reading the book 'Can't Hurt Me' by David Goggins, there were three things I promised myself I would do. Thing No. 1 was to climb this hill ten times in a day. Nobody had ever climbed Malayatoor hill ten times consecutively. Some people could do it. But no one had ever bothered.

This had happened a few months before I got into running. In April 2017, I tried climbing this hill in one go but had to stop twice midway because I almost fainted. That stayed as a bad experience in my mind. If you let such experiences remain as they are, they will be added to your list of fears.

The universe constantly gives us chances to overcome ourselves and become so much more than we ever thought we could be. On any given day, most people have a lot of ideas going through their minds. All the things you see before you now were either invented or accomplished by people brave enough to hold onto their so-called insane ideas. They did not let go of those thoughts, no matter what everyone else said. After reading the book 'Can't Hurt Me,' I honestly believed that I could do anything if I put my body and soul into it.

Auspicious start at 3am

So there I was at the base of Malayatoor hill during Easter week. At other times of the year, this place looked dark and deserted. Today it felt like Christmas night. All of the lamp-posts were turned on.

Overcoming Obstacles

"OM Sahana Vavatu Sahanau Bhunaktu

Saha Viryam Karavavahai Tejasvi Navaditamastu

Ma Vidvishavahai

OM Shanti Shanti Shantihi"

"Om, May we all be protected May we all be nourished

May we work together with great energy

Enlighten our path, with no violence

Om, peace (in divine forces), peace (in nature), peace (in me)"

I recite that before every run or obstacle to have a strong start.

Right from the beginning, something did not feel right. There was a funny feeling in my left knee, where it had dislocated earlier. Regardless of that, the first repetition was done in under an hour. Whenever I got back to the base of the hill where my car was parked, I restocked my hydration bag and got some nutrition in. Being the fool I was, all I had was some oranges, kiwi, apples and cashew nuts. Today was the first time I ate apples during an activity, and they did not sit well in the stomach. So I stopped having those. At the end of every rep, I thanked God thrice. The second rep took the same time.

Rep number 3 took 1 hour and 15 mins. That funny feeling in the knee was not so funny now. A sharp knee pain made me cry out loud. I took my first break mid-rep. Seated on a boulder, I started imagining the worst-case scenario.

Would I have to do this again some other day?

Before arriving at a logical answer, I got up and started moving again.

I had been keeping in constant communication with my wife, who was at home. Every wife has plenty of emotional support to offer. That makes them unique. With the knee pain increasing in intensity, my prediction of completing ten reps in 13 hours had gone to waste. After rep no.5, I informed her that my expected time of getting back home was unknown.

Eight hours after the start, I texted her that rep no.6 was completed. By now, the left knee had become too painful to bend. It was the moment in the day where the pain was at its worst. How the heck am I going to do four more reps in this condition?

I had to do the unthinkable.

The unthinkable was to keep the painful leg straight and use my bendable right knee to move up. And that had to be done to the top. And on the way down, I had to bend my good knee first and place the painful leg at a lower step without bending it.

"If this is what it takes to finish this, then so be it!" I thought.

My heartbeat was also way higher than it should have been. Every hundred metres or so, I was forced to sit down.

"What the heck is happening to my body?" "Is it breaking down from the excess stress?" "Will I die?"

These thoughts started to flood the mind as I was resting at the top during rep no. 7. It was the most tiring thing I had ever experienced in my entire life. It had been 12 hours since the whole thing began. How on earth am I going to do three more reps?

It was in this moment of total weakness that help came from the heavens. And it came in the form of a priest. While seated on a step with my head bent into my hands, I saw a priest slowly making his way in my direction.

"I have seen you repeatedly climbing today. What are you up to?" the priest inquired in a friendly tone.

"I am doing it ten times, Father", I replied.

"Why ten times? Is it some atonement?" he asked.

"No, Father. I'm doing it just because I want to." I replied.

"I am so tired. I do not know how I'm going to do three more reps." I said. "Don't worry. It will happen" the priest assured me with the most gentle smile.

On the way down, any slight bending of the left knee caused the pain to shoot back up again.

Rep no. 7 was done.

Desperate for some salted lime water, I had that from a nearby stall. Looking back, that was the most intelligent thing I did that day. Apart from the knee pain, rep no. 8 felt better. My heartbeat felt normal, and I no longer needed to rest often. Later on, I came to know that the irregular heartbeats were due to salt deficiency. It was the salt intake that brought me back to normal. My knee felt infinitely better too. This was the second miracle. I was absolutely stunned by this change. Instead of wasting time questioning it, I was thankful for it. I thanked whoever or whatever was watching over me.

I celebrated the relatively pain-free rep no.8 with one more salted lime water. Only two more reps remained now. At the juice stall, a dad and his little daughter approached me. The little girl was partially hiding behind her father's legs. She could not stop smiling. Like that priest, the man also asked me what I was doing, as he had seen me scaling the hill multiple times.

Before rep no.9, I texted my wife that today was turning out to be a beautiful day. The heart felt fine. The knee felt better.

I could feel the insides of the left knee but could still keep moving.

It was somewhere around this time I remembered the immortal words of David Goggins.

"I don't stop when I'm tired.

I stop when I'm done."

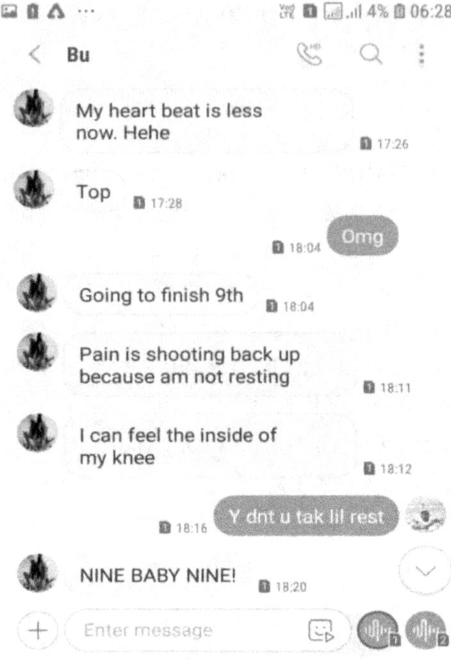

Text messages between wife and me

Pretty soon, I was on my tenth and final rep. Steps were built into the highest parts of the hill where the statue of St. Thomas was housed inside a glass cage. Just like my wife asked me, I ran my way up those 40 something steps on the last ascent. Without taking the proper time to rest, I downed a few mouthfuls of water from the hydration bag. Big mistake!

As the water went down the throat, gases emitted from the stomach were on their way up. With water unable to go down and air unable to go up, I must have choked for about five seconds until I vomited everything out. But that was ok. No harm done.

Finally, after being on Malayatoor Hill for over 17 hours, I completed ten repetitions despite all the obstacles that had to be gone through. Though I had imagined jumping in joy when this would be done, I was emotionless in reality. I didn't jump. I didn't smile. I said thanks to God five times in my mind and quietly got into my car and drove away.

I realized quite a few things that day.

I realized that there is great strength in suffering. Though your body may go through a temporary hardship, your mind will come out of it infinitely stronger. Once you set your mind onto something, then the only outcome is victory.

I realized that the human body would find a way to perform and release its inbuilt painkillers even at its worst. That knee pain never came back once I got into the car.

And I realized that none of us are alone on our journey. There will always be people who are attracted to our efforts and acknowledge them. Like that priest, a dozen others approached to ask me the same question. Each time someone talked to me, it was a sign from above telling me I was on the right path. Most of us believe that our energy is like a battery. We feel there is nothing more to give once we have used up all the power we think we have.

The truth is far from that.

Plenty of power pockets will appear once you change your mindset.

SOLO SUN RUN

I looked up.

The sun was still shining seductively at me. There were no clouds to mask her shine. I looked down.

My watch showed 3pm.

It was one of the hottest days in Kerala in the month of April 2019. There were at least 50 students on the track as well as off it to cheer me on. By kilometre 34, I could not even do a few hundred meters of running without cramping my abdominal muscles in between. It was then I began to seriously question myself "How on earth am I going to complete this in time?"

I have always wanted to do a fundraiser for a great cause. The idea must have slowly grown inside me after watching Hollywood movies since childhood. Movies like 'Freedom Writers' have definitely contributed to the feeling. Back in the day, when I was the Program Officer of the National Service Scheme unit of my college, I had organized a fundraiser for dialysis patients of MOSC hospital in Kolenchery. My uncle, the late Cleetus D'cruz who was a dialysis patient himself, posthumously inspired me to do this. It is strange how some people even after death continue to inspire the living. Years of being on the bottle had taken a toll on his kidneys. Eventually both of them failed and every week he had to undergo a dialysis to stay alive. He did that for months on end before his body could not take it anymore.

In 2013, as I was on my way home from work, an idea aroused in me. "Why not do something for those dialysis patients at that hospital?"

After meeting with the Head of Nephrology department Dr. Kishore S Dharan, he gladly welcomed the idea. With Viswajyothi College of Engineering & Technology having over 2500 students and 250 employees, a tidy sum could be raised. The NSS unit went on to collect Rs. 51,000 which would help 10 needy patients to perform dialysis three times.

This was the doctor's letter of gratitude.

Dear Mr Jibby,

Greetings from Kolenchery.

Let me thank the NSS unit, students and staff of Viswajyothi College of Engineering and Technology for the great gesture of love and care towards the poor dialysis patients at MOSC Medical College, Kolenchery. This is a great step that would help these patients who struggle to continue dialysis that is absolutely essential for continuation of their life. We have given the money for 10 patients who are poor and have limited finances.

Let me once again thank you and also looking forward for further cooperation in future. Let me also invite you to visit the dialysis unit and have a look at the procedure and activities in the dialysis unit.

With best Regards

Dr Kishore S Dharan MD, DM (Vellore) Professor and HOD

Department of Nephrology MOSC Medical College Kolenchery, Kochi

Kerala, India

Even though I had initiated the whole thing, it never felt like a proper fundraiser to me because it was fairly easy. All I had to do was to remind everyone in the college to donate.

In November of 2018, I came up with something else.

"Why not raise funds from my college by running a solo marathon in the hottest month of the year?"

The beneficiary would be Emmanuel Children's Home in Thodupuzha. This orphanage was very dear to me as it was one of the first orphanages I visited as a Program Officer of the NSS unit. The idea was shared with my wife. Then it went into a deep sleep for a while. Four months later after doing a couple of marathons and the Vagamon Ultrail 60k, it resurfaced.

After watching an online motivation video titled "Through Hell', I finally decided to talk to my college Principal about the charity run. I still remember the nervousness I felt before presenting the idea.

What if the Principal says no? That would have shattered my dream.

I took special care to use strategic words in the conversation like "Sir, if YOU can permit this…" and "This has been my DREAM for the last 6 months…" Fortunately, he agreed.

The Marathon Gods have given me one more opportunity to experience the fun of 42.2kms.

The Director of Emmanuel Children's Home, Thomas Brother, was surprised when I told him about the fundraiser. The auspicious date for the run was the hottest time of the year with a daytime temperature of 34 degree celsius. The venue would be the open football ground of the college. The starting time would be 9 am. It was not exactly the typical starting time for a marathon. I had to finish it by 4.30pm as that was the functioning time of the college. Seven and half hours to run 42.2kms seemed do-able. But to do it in summer and in the sun should be an unforgettable experience. And I wanted to do it on a regular working day of the college so that it was there for all to see. My colleagues insisted on starting early before sunrise to escape the heat.

"What fun was there in doing the already done?" I would reply.

The YouTube audio by Sadhguru 'Organize Your Mind and Anything You Wish Will Happen' was played on repeat whenever

I had time to myself. So much was at risk. There was a good possibility that I could get a heatstroke and the run would turn in the direction of a hospital. I could end up being a fool. My colleagues could make fun of me. My students could laugh behind my back.

Oh, and one more thing.

42.2kms would be run as repeats on a 200 metre track chalked on the ground. Yes, you guessed it right.

211 loops would have to be done to complete that distance.

This was the adopted mentality during the run.

"The only way to not get burned is to become fire."

So, on the very sunny and very warm 6th of May 2019 at 9am, I started my 'Solo Sun Marathon' at the start of the whistle by the Physical Education instructor of the college. The aim was to run 5 loops, i.e. 1 km, continuously and then walk for 1 loop. Then repeat the procedure again. A student was in charge of manually keeping count of the distance I had covered. After the first kilometre, I proceeded to the umbrella set up beside the track for hydration and refreshments. There were oranges and kiwis for nutrition. It was set up by the students of the NSS (National Service Scheme) unit of the college. I could do only three loops before I had to find the comfort of the umbrella again. The heat got to me earlier than I had anticipated.

What am I saying! It got to me almost immediately.

On the bright side, even though I had planned to run this by myself, the faculty and some of the students were there to support me. Almost all of the students who came to see the live event accompanied me even if it were for a few loops. Three of the final year NSS students decided they would do their first ever half marathon (21.1 kms) then and there. They rested whenever I rested. Among them was a competition-level body builder by the name of Mr. Paulson Joseph. He held the title of Mr. Idukki in 2018. (Idukki being a district in Kerala) Having a muscular body may have helped him all along but today it was disastrous for his run. His thigh muscles kept giving him a hard time by cramping every now and then. But he kept on.

I covered 14km in two hours. It took me that long to come to terms with the hot climate. Or was it with the arrival of the Head of Electronics & Communication Engineering department Mr. Jose P Varghese that eased my run? Mr. Jose P Varghese was attacked by polio virus very early in life. He had to use two crutches from then on. It was inspiring to see him walk two loops with a kerchief on his head. He had to use two crutches from then on. It was inspiring to see him walk two loops with a kerchief on his head. A loudspeaker was also arranged by the students to blast some high energy music into the air.

Students supporting the event

Everyone who came there wanted a piece of the action. Faculty, students, lab technicians, sweepers and even the vice-principal did numerous loops with me. And that kept me going.

After 3 hours and 15 minutes, the half marathon part was done. I nearly collapsed on a chair under the umbrella and had a moment of relief that the halfway was done. Students would pour water on my head and upper back each time I took a break. Paulson went on to complete 105 loops. All of us cheered him on in his final loop. It was an epic moment in the run. Seeing a bodybuilder who never took to running complete his maiden 21kms was a moment in time worth remembering. The other two boys also did their intended half marathon. They did it wearing converse shoes and a college uniform.

By kilometre 34, I was hydrating more than I should have. The consequence was frequent occurrence of side-stitch in the stomach. There was not one part of my stomach that did not cramp. The middle, the sides, the upper muscles all took their turn in turning my runs into walks. If this went on, I would not be able to make it when the college closes for the day. That made me stop drinking water altogether.

Only a few minutes to 4.30 pm remained and I needed to do 2.2 kms. Fearing that the college buses would leave before I finished this, I knew I had to change my mentality. Something inside me switched. With eyes fixated on the ground, I had to go to a place of intense concentration in my mind. I ran the last 11 loops non-stop. This was the longest continuous run I had done throughout the event. It was announced through the mic that I had one more lap to go. The final footsteps of the run were completed by 4.15pm when I ran through the ribbon at the finishing point.

It was done.

I took over the mic to address the gathering of faculty and students at the ground. I thanked everyone and told them that this could not have happened if it was not for the constant support from my fellow runners. And now was time for everyone to contribute for the well-being of the orphanage. Pictures and selfies were taken with staff and students alike to cherish the memory.

The solo run was not so solo after all.

A month later, with the collection fund in hand, I walked into the office of the Emmanuel Children's Home at Thodupuzha.

Thomas Brother and his wife were present. The lady burst into tears when I told them that the event raised one lakh rupees.

I will never forget that moment.

What you can do and cannot do is not for any person or any climate or any circumstance to decide.

It's all on you.

Faculty doing a few rounds of their own

William Ernest Henley That night, I went to bed with the most incredible feeling I have ever had in my life.

"You are the master of your fate. You are the captain of your soul.

DON'T FORGET!

Now, who could have said that and why?

Being the once-upon-a-time dislocated knee person I was, my parents and I were never eye-to-eye with my running. They could not come to terms with me running at noon or going on long bike rides. Before every marathon event, I would meet them the previous night to tell them about it and seek their blessings.

In November 2017, when I told them I would be doing the Spice Coast Half Marathon, they said, "Don't you know that you have a bad knee?"

In December 2017, when I told them I would be doing my first ever full marathon at Trivandrum Midnight Marathon, they said, "Don't you know that you have a bad knee?"

Guess what they said in January 2019 when I told them I would be doing my first ever ultra marathon at Vagamon Ultrail 60K?

The same.

Though I was a 33-year-old adult at the time, such a response from them was devastating for me. It sank my heart. Parents are supposed to encourage the dreams of a child. Not just in childhood.

But blaming them was of no use. How can you judge a person who had limited knowledge about a particular thing at the time? Running long distances have been admired when others do it but frowned upon when your loved ones do it. Most parents want their children to avoid risks and play it safe. And as for me, the desire to change their mindset was even more.

So what do you do at times you receive such negativity in life? You turn it upside down and use it as your fuel. You use it to drive your engines. Prove them wrong. Enlighten them. Broaden their view.

There were days when I would go running in the mornings and evenings as well. When dad came to know about it, he certainly was not pleased.

"Are you trying to create a Guinness world record?"

"Don't forget that you have a wife and child."

This was what dad said. This is what most people say about those who think out-of-the-box.

Usually, I am very calm on the outside. I have learned not to let adversities in life disturb me. But when it comes to hearing words like these, all the calmness goes away. In a moment of anger, I shouted whatever words I could think of at the moment.

The coming Sunday was a long-run day. As per the training plan mentioned in the book 'The Cool Impossible' by Eric Orton, there was one hour and twenty minutes of running to be done. Going into this with a disheartened mentality would not have done me any good.

Luckily, I found a motivational video online by Walter Bond named 'Shark Mentality'. Whenever Walter Bond came at particular crossroads in his life, his dad intervened to uplift Walter's spirit. Walter went on to play in the National Basketball Association. Just before the Sunday run, I played it on loop and engraved those words into my mind.

Armed with the new 'shark mentality', I set out on the run. It had to be continuous without any stops in between. I was supposed to cover a distance of 18 kilometers that morning. Walter senior's words to his son, "Do you believe you are an NBA player?" echoed in my mind with every step. What followed was that I was able to run 18 kilometers as expected and was relatively pain-free. But with just three more kilometers for a half marathon, the temptation to attempt it was irresistible. And I went for it.

I did my fastest half marathon that day in 1 hour and 52 minutes with a little bit of luck, a lot of motivation, and a huge smile. So I guess I have my dad to thank. I could not have done this without him.

A THOUSAND TIMES

After reading the book 'Can't Hurt Me' by David Goggins, I decided I would complete three things at any cost.

Thing no.1: Scale the 1000 feet Malayatoor Hill 10 times in a single day.

Thing no.2: Climb Malayatoor Hill once, do a non-stop Half Marathon of 21.1 km and then climb it again.

Thing no.3: Do 1000 push-ups in one day.

The first attempt at thing no.3 was a fantastic failure. Even with no proper training, I could still do 899 push-ups. Hence, the word 'fantastic.' The form I used was incorrect. The entire load goes into the shoulder sockets if one does push-ups with arms extended away from the body. Sooner or later, they will be completely sore. My case was no different. By 11.30 pm, I had to quit. I was relieved that my suffering finally came to an end and sought the comfort of my bed. But that was when the mind began to suffer. This feeling of incompleteness was lodged in the back of my mind and would go on to last nine months before I found the right opportunity to attempt it once again.

In the words of Elon Musk, "Things may not work out in the beginning, but eventually, they will and I'm going to keep trying until it does." Elon Musk is not known for executing any push-ups. But when it comes to executing thoughts in his head, no one does it better than him. During times when you doubt yourself, those words will surely change your perspective and your actions.

September 1, 2019 Attempt No.2

This was the perfect day to suffer. It was a Sunday morning. It is said that God made the Universe in six days and rested on the seventh. No rest for me on this Sunday. The wife was still asleep. At 7.30 am, I began the push-ups on an empty stomach. It was an enthusiastic start. Like

the last time, I decided to break the thousand push-ups into sets of ten. This time, I tried doing it every 5 minutes. Not too hard, is it? Well, it was going to be.

Let's address the first question. Will I be called crazy?

Yes.

Now the second question. Am I stupid? No.

Because I know exactly how this will benefit me once I get this done. Those who label me crazy are also the ones who cannot imagine themselves doing it.

The world needs doctors, lawyers, engineers and so on. It also needs adventurers with people crazy enough to push the preconceived limits of the mind and body a little further.

The first 500 push-ups went relatively well. The shocker came when my triceps failed at the 479th push-up and I fell on my chest. With 500 more to go, this was not a good sign. Of course, I did have breakfast and lunch in moderate quantities. So it was not from the lack of nutrition. By now, the lactic acid accumulating in my biceps was starting to build up.

At 3.45 pm, the count was 650. I also had to visit my in-laws that day. After spending a few minutes exchanging pleasantries at their home, I went to use the restroom on the floor above. It would be the fourth time I had to go since the day began.

Oh, I forgot to mention that I was going through a mild case of diarrhea that day.

Earlier that day, after waking up, I had to run to the restroom. My stomach did not feel right. Though I did not go running, exercise, or eat out the previous day, I could not determine why this illness affected me. With this new development, there was a decision to be made. Should I press on with the push-up thing or postpone it to another day?

"When you turn excuses into efforts, those are the magical moments in your life."

I did not want my statement to be, "I am not doing this because I had diarrhea." I wanted to say, "I am doing this despite it!" Intervals of high-intensity stomach pains which lasted a few seconds would come and go. They were so painful that my wife could hear me in agony from the next room. Even my 2-year-old daughter came and stroked her tiny little hands on my stomach to comfort me. Life will always hurl obstacles at you whenever you embark on something out of the ordinary. That's just how it is. I waited for those pain-free intervals to resume the push-ups. This went all the way up to the first 500 ones. It was only from noon that I began feeling a lot better.

Your body will heal itself if you set your mind to it.

Actually, I was counting on this to happen. Now, coming back to the moment where I was at my in-law's house. The time was six in the evening, and I completed another 60 push-ups in the dark hall upstairs. I love doing things in the dark. There is nothing else in the darkness. There is just you and that voice in your head. It is the perfect place to focus all your effort. Nova would occasionally come up and talk to me. She even enquired how my stomach was doing.

After getting back to my home and having supper, it was half-past nine, and the count was 800. My arms were so high on lactic acid that I had to bring ten reps at a time down to 5 reps. Every ten or fifteen minutes, I would do it, stretch and massage my arms. For the first push-up of those five reps to happen, I had to use all my might. It was like overcoming tremendous friction in my arms. I could feel the veins on my neck and forehead ready to burst. The question of whether or not I would get a stroke popped into my mind. I knew I had to keep up this pace or I would not finish the whole thing in 24 hours before 7.30 am the next day. There was no easy way out of this.

"Suffer it out, Jibby."

My wife and kid were fast asleep by 10.30 pm. It was time to call for backup.

David Goggins, Les Brown and Elon Musk.

There is not a single day that goes by when I do not hear their voice. You only have so much energy and when the going gets tough, you need others to carry you further. I moved the speakers into the room and played their inspirational stories on loop. Energy and zest renewed, I got back into rhythm. Being by myself and with no one to break my focus, I could now do 20 – 25 push-ups every hour. I tested to see if sleeping for half an hour would reduce the pain. It did not.

Good Morning Jibby!

It was midnight. Sunday now became Monday. One hundred fifty more to go. I desperately wanted to have my wife beside me to find some comfort and to massage my arms. But looking back, I am glad she did not wake up. In finding comfort, I would have lost valuable time. I chose not to be comfortable. I did not want to soften.

01.30 am: Push-up no. 900.

03.30 am: 950.

"You didn't sleep?!" asked my wife at 5 in the morning. She said my loud cry woke her up from the other room. I smiled back and replied with five more push-ups on the floor.

By 6 am, 995 was completed.

After having a hot breakfast, I got in the last five before leaving for work at 6.30 am. 1000 push-ups in 23 hours despite no sleep, no training, and a sour stomach.

THE THIRD TIME

My wife got pregnant once again. It was not a planned one. Of course, we could not say no to God's blessing. But after two months, that ended in a miscarriage too. Doctors told us that it should not have happened. It was because the part of her uterus that caused the miscarriage should have been strengthened with Nova's delivery two years ago.

It was her third failed pregnancy. It feels too much, doesn't it?

How can one define 'too much'? Because there are people who have gone through a lot worse.

Once again, she moved to her parent's place to get some quality rest and recovery. This was in July of 2019. She stayed there for a month with my daughter, who was two years old at the time. This was one of the most nerve-racking months in my life too.

Since we had a home to ourselves, I did not want to stay at my parent's place, a couple of houses away. A home without your wife and child is not exactly home. But for the most part, I could manage on my own. Going on early morning runs took place as usual. I could not let the thought of a lost child affect that area of my life. Running was therapeutic for me. It has always given me a massive relief in times of stress. Since I was also on a month-long vacation from work, I used this free time to enroll in a PG Diploma course on Industrial Automation.

Every morning, I would wake up at 5 am. Go for a 45-minute run. Cook the same breakfast every day, which consists of banana-puttu, omelets and fried chicken breasts. Take the bus to attend the Industrial Automation course 15kms away. The morning session lasted one and a half hours. Then attend IELTS (International English Language Test) classes on the floor below from 10 am to 2 pm. Go for the second round of the Industrial Automation course from 2 pm to 4.30 pm. Get back home by 5.30 pm. Do strength training for an hour. I Ate supper from my parent's home, which was nearby. Then I went to bed by 11 pm, which ensured that I got a six-hour sleep before the next day's run.

I did that for a month.

On most days, I was able to cruise through this hectic schedule. On other days the cumulative effect of the stress at class, being away from my family, losing a child, the running, the workouts, and the silence at home frustrated me.

My mind felt paralyzed.

"What was the point of doing all these?" I questioned myself. But I held on.

Life has a way of helping me find a shoulder to hang on to during times of desperation.

It was also the time when I found motivational talks of Les Brown and Arnold Schwarzenegger online. Every day during the one-hour lunch break at class, I would listen to stories on trials and tribulations Les Brown had to offer from his life. That helped me understand that there is a way out of anything in life. It helped me learn that no problem is too deep and that no pain is too great.

You can overcome it all.

On most days, I would be the first to arrive for class and the last one to leave. I had to make the best use of the one month of absence I had from work. It was a three-month course.

I did it in 30 days.

Life forced me to do that.

Sometimes 'the only way' becomes 'your way' when there is 'no other way.'

I also got through the busy schedule, thanks to Arnold.

Back in the day, Arnold used to work out for 5 hours in the gym. But there was no money in bodybuilding then. So he worked in construction to make ends meet. He also went to college. Because he wanted to be an actor, he found the time for that too. Arnold went to acting classes four times a week from 8 pm to midnight.

If he could do all that, then I could do all this too.

Whenever the day became too hard, I worked out equally harder.

Bad things have happened to good people. One cannot control that. But you need not be defined by it. Look around. Successful people leave clues. These are clues on managing your life and doing all the things you still want to.

But these clues are not for free. Time and effort are the cost.

With those two in your pocket, you can climb the highest mountains with the heaviest of burdens.

THE IRON MINDSET

There comes an age

    when fate may seem too cruel,

With nickels and dimes in wage

    I refuse to let it rule.

In locks and in chain

    my steps may falter,

All dusk ends with dawn

    I pray for it thereafter.

My body may grow weak

    it cannot harm my mind,

When the road ahead looks bleak

    I will dig up every strength I can find.

From every thorn and nail

    my legs may kneel,

I will go on, never to fail

    for tomorrow I will heal.

I will rise, O I will rise

    to mountainous heights untold,

With steady steps and surprise

    to see what each peak shall unfold.

The sea I swim

    may boil and scald,

My voyage though grim

    will not be stalled.

And when I have done it

    with my back on the shore,

I know I'll be strong and fit

    enough to do it once more!

I USED TO RUN AND STILL DO

I am not a PB (Personal Best) guy. I am a newbie guy. I like to do new runs, new distances and new elevations. Overcoming new obstacles fuels me. Shaving a few minutes off the clock in marathons does not seem that motivating. The only reason I did the Spice Coast full marathon a second time was because I told myself I would never do flat road marathons again. But that is precisely why you should do it once again.

Do the things you said you would never do. Get inside that suffering and make it your normal. Then you will undoubtedly find a new you in you that will change your mindset. Suddenly all the problems in life will not seem so problematic anymore.

The day started out sweaty. It had rained the previous night. This is Cochin, and there is no escaping the humidity. Accept it and face it. With one final kiss from my wife, I got to the launching line. The wife was all set to launch next for her very first half-marathon.

One runs in space and the other on earth

She had been training for two weeks (even though she was on her periods). This is why it is so important to do the things that you do. You never know who you are going to inspire. I would never have made it this far if not for all those inspirational characters who found their way at critical points in my life.

The objective was to run continuously between the aid stations. That went well only till kilometer 30, which I was able to do in 3 hrs. It was practically a miracle compared to the previous year, where my lower back troubled me from kilometer 15. Shortly after the 30km mark, the 4.00-hour pacer bus went by.

In a pacer-bus system, a group of runners wanting to finish the run, say in 4 hours, will run behind a leader who can do it in 4 hours.

I thought the back pain would go away after a while. This full marathon was not long enough for my body to adjust to it. Therefore, I had to rely on those pain relief sprays from kilometer 34. In another part of Kochi, my wife's hands were swelling up during the run. That subsided when the race volunteers poured ice water at an aid station.

After a while, I saw the 4.30 (4 hours 30 mins) pacer bus approaching. The only thing was that the passengers, i.e., the co-runners, were missing. Only the bus driver was there. Since that was the time I intended to finish in, I happily told him, "I will join you."

But he replied, "I am 10 minutes behind pace as I got hit by a bike. His Plan B was to run-walk the remaining distance.

What a soul! Hit by a bike and still pushing on. This world needs more people like him.

In the previous Spice Coast Marathon, my calf muscles cramped a lot. This year it was surprising that it never even came close to happening even while changing my socks. Tempo runs do help during training.

My run, which began at 3.30 in the morning, ended after 4 hours and 44 minutes. I improved by half an hour compared to the previous year. The wife did her maiden 21.1kms in 3 hours and 15 mins. Mom did the 7km fun run in 1 hour. Dad walked it in 1 hour and 15 mins.

Mom and dad used to be my biggest demotivators whenever I went on long runs. Making them participate changed their view. Our run ended there. But unlike us, the real heroes were still on the course, especially those half-marathoner guys and girls, old and young. Some of them were still behind the full marathoners. I am not sure how their story ended. But I bet they never gave up.

Do not look to the left. Do not look to the right.

Nor look who is ahead of you or who is behind you. Just look within.

Dig deep. Keep pushing.

So why should people run? Why not?

Why not you?

And why not now?

Get started. Get going.

As children, we loved running. We even found happiness in getting breathless after each run. What happened to us?

LOOP DE LOOP

(The following run had been attempted by an unprofessional and you should try it at home)

The human body is an interesting piece of parts put together, each working with the other to achieve a common goal. The body tries to survive, to push on even during conditions you thought you would never be able to go through. Thousands of years ago, we only had our bodies and our mindset to survive each day as hunter-gatherers. But for most of us, that life has become obsolete, and we no longer need to push ourselves. Money has made matters easier. Our bodies have become comfortable beyond measure. But the thing is this.

Endurance running is one way to toughen you up. With marathons and ultra-marathons popping up every day, there are plenty of opportunities to do that. But to have a unique mindset, you need to do unique things.

"The more comfortable the body gets, the weaker the mind becomes."

So on the 22nd of December 2019, with barely three weeks left for Vagamon Ultrail 90K, I decided it would be the right time to run 3kms at the start of every hour for 18 hrs. Three simple kilometers in a village on a road with no elevation. How tough can it be? But repeating the same thing on the same loop in the same way for three-quarters of a day would, without doubt, be challenging. I named it the 'Loop de Loop.' There is an ultra marathon in the US called 'Last Man Standing' where runners would repeat a 4-mile loop every hour until they could not take it anymore. Only the last runner who did not quit would get the title of 'Last Man Standing'. Everyone else would technically be 'Did-not-finish.' That was where the idea for my run arose.

The idea of a race or a run is to have a starting line and a finishing line, however short or long it may be. And you can find satisfaction once you get to the finishing point. But the Loop de Loop will not be like that. You will find no pleasure once you get to the finishing line because you will have to do it all over again in the next hour. And the hour after that and again and again.

I had already done the 12 hr - 4km version of this last year as part of training for Vagamon Ultrail 60K. The cut-off time for Vagamon Ultrail 90K was 18 hrs. Hence, running the Loop de Loop for the same period at a reduced mileage and effort would be an excellent opportunity to learn more about the body.

At 6 am, I was outside my home, all set to begin. The compound wall gate of my house was the starting point. The climate was cool. At an average pace of about 5.15 mins/km, I completed the first loop in a time of about 16 mins. Then got back to the same starting line, which was also the finishing line. The aid station was my home. Initially, I watched a movie until the time for the next loop began. The 2nd loop began at 7 am. It was beautiful seeing my 3-year-old daughter at the doorstep with a plate of avocado, dried kiwi slices and dates after loop number 3. By noon, the climate was the opposite of cool. One-third of the route did not have any tree shade. The weather forecast said, "it is 34 degrees but feels like 37".

"So what?" I said to myself.

Nobody promised me that this was going to be easy. You do not pray for anything to become easier. Instead, you should be praying to find more strength. Keep moving forward. Know that whatever suffering you are facing is just temporary. Everything will make sense once the journey is complete.

The sun is life-giving and life-draining at the same time. No longer was I in the mood to watch movies in between loops. I would come home, strip myself of all the clothes, lie down tired and sweaty on the yoga mat. By the time the minute hand reached 12 on the clock, I had come to my senses to begin the next loop. During the sunny runs, I imagined all the legends and martyrs throughout history who went through unspeakable pain and torture to stand for what they believed. That helped me imagine how comparatively relaxed my state was. Sometimes one has to imagine absurd things to get things done. I visualized that I was a funnel through which all the energy in the universe flowed. That kept feeding my mind with more power.

I chose to have fruits the entire afternoon and went for peanut butter only after sunset. After the 6 pm run, the blister on my little toe had come back. The skin on that part was still soft after the Spice Coast Marathon three weeks back. This time it was bleeding inside the blister. I tried to run the next loop with duct tape on it. That only made matters worse. So I removed it. The blister spread to the sides and the top of the toe to form a cute red bubble.

Nice.

It was loop 18 now, the last one. This was the only round I could not run continuously. Side stitch was the issue. The stomach muscles were cramping heavily. In the past, that always subsided in a minute. This time it did not. So I decided to walk the final loop. It was a good time to recall the day's events. I was so tired that I kept falling asleep while moving. The Christmas lights and stars that adorned the residential homes on the route made me sleepier.

The run that began at 6 am ended after nearly 18 hours, with 30 minutes to midnight. That's 3.4km per loop for 18 loops, adding to a total of 61.2 km. The weighing scale showed I was 3 kgs lighter at the end of the day.

So, why do it?

Life has thrown so many obstacles at me. Fortunately, each time, I was able to come back with a bang. And when they do keep coming, I need to be in the proper mindset to go through them. To not slip or lose my footing and to keep my eyes on the target.

I want to have an iron mindset. Doing challenging runs helps me to keep that mindset. Eighteen times it felt like I had died that day. But eighteen times, I was also reborn, with a whole new mentality. That is the reward.

If it takes a long time to achieve, it will take a long time to go away. Nutrition after each loop:

Loop 1: Peanut butter 2: Nothing

3: An orange

4: Half avocado + 1 dried kiwi slice

5: I forgot to eat while watching the movie 6: 1 dates + 2 dried kiwi slice

7: Watermelon

8: Watermelon + 1 kiwi fruit

9: 1 orange + 1 cucumber

10: Half avocado + dried kiwi 11,12,13,14: melon + orange 15,16: peanut butter

17: Nothing

18: Steamed carrots and broccoli

Total distance completed

THE RUN AFTER THE RUN

(A one big explanation for not completing Vagamon Ultrail 90K)

206 kilometers. I hope that matters. I hope that this mileage in training runs done in the previous month will set me up for a successful 90K finish in the third edition of Vagamon Ultrail on January 11th 2020. Having successfully completed the 60K category of the ultra marathon in the previous year, covering 90 kilometers with a net ascent of 2848m in a cut-off time of 18 hours did not seem terrifying.

The run began at 5am. It was both chilly and windy. This was the very first time I had used a headlamp for an official event in the morning. Unlike last year, I kept conversations with fellow runners to a minimum as I wanted to finish the whole run in 15 hrs. This is one of the downsides of being too goal-oriented.

The first 28 km of the course had more elevation compared to last year's edition. I was able to do reasonably well till this portion of the run leading up to the first cut-off point and rest area at Amma's Hotel. This place would also serve as the same cut-off point at 56K. Idlis and sweet potatoes were available here. Skipping the idli and having just half a sweet potato was the first of the many awful decisions I made that day. I wasted time accessing my drop bag to change my underwear and my running top from a full-sleeved to a sleeveless one. The part

"Everybody has a plan until you get punched in the mouth."

– Mike Tyson

between the 28K and 56K had both rocky and grassy plains. So I had a change of shoe from the road/trail shoe to the Kalenji XT7 trail shoe. Looking back, that was the only wise decision I made that day. From here on things went downhill. Not literally but physically.

Vagamon Ultrail 90K seemed to shift to a whole new gear now. The sun was way up in the sky and the climate was hotter than last year. I kept going out of breath. My heartbeat was at an all-time high whenever I tried to run. Even on the downhills. My lower back felt weak and painful. This usually happens to me after some 30km of running. All the Eluid Kipchoge, Mo, Farah, James Dunne core and hip strengthening workouts I practiced from YouTube did not do me any good during the run.

"What more could I have done to not deserve this?" I asked myself.

From the very first full marathon back in 2017 to this day, this lower back issue has chased me no matter whatever I tried to strengthen it.

"You should have had a better breakfast, not skipped lunch and had a lot more nutrition from the aid-stations!" I scolded myself

The fatigue was slowly but surely catching up to me. And now it raised its head in the form of breathlessness. In the pursuit of becoming faster on the trail, I had given lesser importance to caloric intake. Because this was more or less the same nutrition I had when I completed Malnad 80K two months back.

"You should have done more elevation training!" I scolded myself again.

The nine day Christmas holidays I got were spent doing meaningless runs on flat roads. Only once did I train for elevation by hiking up and down the 1000 ft Malayatoor hill thrice in a row.

It was around mid-day when I noticed a passenger flight making a climb in the sky. I imagined the pilots seated comfortably inside their air-conditioned cockpit doing nothing but pushing the throttle to increase the momentum. Instead, they should be made to run on treadmills for the duration of the flight to power the engines. Why should only we runners suffer while they get to sit back in their seats without breaking a sweat?

One of the last runners to reach the highest points of the race

And now for some good news. The Kalenji XT7 shoe was proving its worth with a 'gorilla grip' on most surfaces. I can recall slipping only once in those shoes. But I hurt my leg when my knee bounced off a rock camouflaged by thick overgrowth on a narrow trail. A little blood did not do much damage, unlike what happened to my friend from Oman, Mr. Viju the Wanderer. He fell twice during the initial stages of the run and had two bloody knees. Viju went on to complete the 90K with only twenty minutes to spare on the clock. Supermen do come in all shapes and sizes.

The run along those multiple peaks at around 35K gave me multiple heart attacks. Shortly after, a fellow runner Mr. Murali from CTC (Chennai Trail Club), happened to run with me. Murali had gone off-course by about 5km in one direction. That was 10 km of extra workout exclusive to Murali. Even he caught up to me. Imagine how bad my condition was. Seeing me in my sorry state, Murali offered me a Fast & Up energy gel. I had been skeptical about these products all along. Will it sit well in my stomach? Will those unnatural sugars do more harm than good? Now was not the time to ponder over such questions. There is a first time for everything. I gladly had them. And boy, was it tasty! The banana and the strawberry flavor, along with the caffeine, all tasted quite good. Though I had salt tablets regularly, another valuable suggestion he made was to consume rock salt from the aid stations.

"Why didn't you think of this earlier, Jibby! It's not rocket science. Didn't you have a similar experience of going out of breath while you were climbing Malayatoor hill ten times?" It was the salt-lime that stabilized my heart rate then.

After the rock-salt intake, things started to get better. At 39km, I was offered another gel at the aid station by the very humble but very strong 100-miler Mithra Kumar. It was an equally tasty berry blast from Unived. After kilometer 44, the back pain was now under control and the fatigue nearly non-existent. Hurray for energy gels!

The next cut-off point was at Amma's hotel at 56km and had to be crossed by 4 pm. The time was now 3.16 pm. The volunteer at the aid station Vijayachandran told me to hurry. And he said it without smiling. With absolutely no idea if I would take the time or what the trail ahead looked like, there was only one way to meet the 56km mark. It was time for the Garuda Run.

It seems silly talking about it now. The Garuda Run is where I spike my beard up, and the brain shouts at all the energy reservoirs to release everything. Self-talk and visualization were the tools.

I kept talking to myself, "You don't know me." and "I'm the hardest person there is."

Now is that true? Probably not.

But at that moment, I had to make that my reality to empower the mind and get the physical switch done.

Next came, "Who did 1000 push-ups in 24 hrs without sleeping?" You did!

"Who stood by as strong as an ox during his wife's third abortion?" You did!

There were no weak moments in that run.

Soon, the entrance to the Pine Forest from the main road was in sight. The walkway was narrow and crowded with tourists. No way I was about to lose precious time navigating my way through the crowd according to their convenience. Instead, I torpedoed through it.

"വഴി! വഴി!" (Give way! Give way!) I yelled at the top of my voice. People moved away just in time as I sped through as fast as I could. At one point, I braked just in time, hitting a lady and lost my balance. The guy next to her gripped me by the shoulder. Unsure if it was to help or slap me, I cried out

"ചേട്ടാ, സത്യമായിട്ടും എനിക്ക് വയ്യ!" (Bro, I am exhausted!)
He let go.

During the speedy downhill run inside the Pine Forest, coordinating between keeping an eye on the ground, the crowd and the trail marker ribbons were no easy task.

At 3.43 pm, I crashed into Amma's hotel. I had made the cut-off.

Only two others made it in time after me.

Realizing the importance of forcing food into the stomach, I had two idlis and sambar from there and used the toilet twice. Half an hour seemed too long to spend in an aid station, and I left in a hurry.

At that moment, I had forgotten to take my headlamp from my supplies bag over there. Game over! It was not permitted for runners to run in the night without headlamps.

By the time I had the brains to realize this blunder, it was already an hour's worth of distance away from Amma's Hotel. No point in going back. No point in going forward. There was only one runner behind me and he did not have a spare lamp or a torch. By then, the race volunteers had transported my supplies bag to the finishing point. The fact that I forgot my headlamp did not shock me. Nor was I angry at myself for it. I was too tired to be shocked or angry. The only comfort I could provide my mind was to cover as much distance as I could before sunset. And then do the remaining distance on a course of my choosing before going to bed. The volunteer at the next aid station offered me his torch, but it was not charged.

By 6.30 pm, it was getting dark, and I decided to quit at a timing station at 64.5 km. My very first DNF (Did-Not-Finish)!

That sounded better than a DSQ (disqualification) further on for going on without a headlamp. I was becoming restless to complete the remaining 25.5k. But before I got the chance, I had to wait a long time. The race volunteers transported me to my place of accommodation Green Palace Residency at around 9 pm. That meant my supplies bag, containing all the running gear (the headlamp, the long-sleeved running top, gels, snack bars and the smartphone), was still at the finishing point at St Thomas LP School. I needed them for 'the run after the run.'

Those who completed the 90K were dropped off from the finishing point to the resort. To get back my bag, I had to catch a ride back in the shuttle vehicle. Taxi cars were unavailable as it was already past 9 pm. During the long wait outside the Green Palace Residency resort office, a runner Lakshmi Thampi, from the 33K fun run category, was kind enough to offer her shawl to the shivering and bent down seated me. I was still in my running outfit. This is the one thing I adore about runners. They are always ready to offer anything they can to help out a fellow runner. It may be their gel, water or even a simple running tip.

After 1 hour out in the cold, I decided it would be better to have my bag delivered to me. At 11.15 pm, it arrived. I could not start running yet because my roomie Mithilesh Kumar had to complete his 90K and return. Running with newly bought zero drop shoes did not work out too well for him. He finished it just in time. Fifteen minutes past midnight, he made it back. After handing over the keys to the room, I left to do the remaining distance.

The distance between Green Palace Residency and Green Line Hotel (where the pre-race briefing was done) is exactly 1 km with an elevation of 54m. 64.5 km on the Ultrail was already done. The remaining distance to complete the 90K would be done here as loops. 12.5 loops would equal 25.5K and that would get the job done.

So why be so stubborn to do it now? Isn't Vagamon 2021 happening?

Yes, there will always be a next time. But I could not let the thought of not running 90K occupy space in my head for a whole year. It is not about the medal. Medals, trophies, mementos and cash prizes are only materialistic gifts you get for the work you have done. It is the work that matters. Nobody can take that away from you.

Moreover, nobody gave me a medal for 1000 push-ups. Nor did I receive any award for supporting my wife in her times of crisis. You do it because you know it makes you a better person. A stronger person. A more peaceful person.

So, here we go again.

I had three dates and a scoop of peanut butter. With a liter of water in the hydration bag, I checked my gear.

H-E-A-D-L-A-M-P check!

Running commenced at 12.21 am on Sunday. I ran on the way down and walked on the ups. Surprised to see the unfamiliar sight of someone running with a headlamp past midnight, some of the vehicles passing by slowed down. The knee pain from hitting that boulder reminded me that it was still there. With not much for fuel other than dates, I had that gel and cereal grain bar from the goodie bag every runner got at the registration. It must have been at least a year since I have eaten a chocolate bar. At 3 am, I got my first yawn since the run began the previous day. It had been 24 hrs and 45 minutes since I had last slept. Finally, the 25.5km part, which has an elevation of 648m (2125 ft), came to an end at 4.14 am with a pace averaged at 9.08 min/km. I texted my wife at home that 90K had been done. She was staying awake for me to finish it and I went to sleep shortly after.

"If you have a chalk, you can draw your finish line."

For the time being, I guess I will have to find peace of mind in those words. This setback has undoubtedly given me something to focus on for the year ahead. Whatever it takes, I will be back for 2021 Vagamon Ultrail 90K.

In the meantime, the only thing to do is wait and train. And train and wait.

P.S: Vagamon 2021 did not happen due to the covid pandemic. See, this is what I said. The future looks uncertain. 'Right now', is all you have.

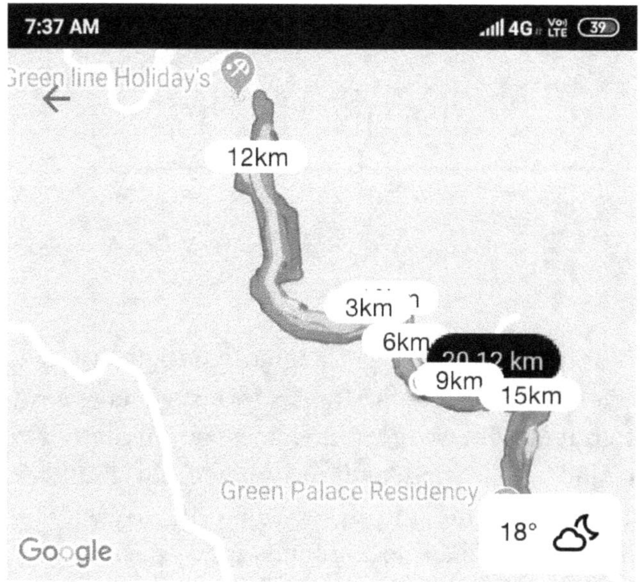

The unofficial 25 km run after the official DNF at 65km

VISITING SAVIO

Pretty Lil Hearts (PLH) is a Chennai-based Non-Governmental Organization run by the youth who believe they have a role to play in the betterment of our world. PLH does various activities such as educating and sponsoring underprivileged children, feeding the needy and empowering the deserving. My affiliation with PLH began in 2015 when I had certain funds for disposal, and Rs.10,000 was donated to support the wonderful activities PLH was doing in Chennai. A student of my college suggested the NGO. He happened to have friends volunteering in PLH. One such volunteer is Savio John. Savio was also the cameraman for my interview for a YouTube channel, 'Kanavu Katchers' (Dream Catchers). Today, he continues to be a very dear friend. After visiting me for the third time, travelling over 600km from Chennai, I wanted to meet with him in his hometown at Salem. But that reason alone was not motivating enough for me to visit him. Luckily, the 3rd edition of Yercaud Hills Ultra (YHU) in February 2020 was happening near Salem, and that left me with no second thoughts. I registered for the 50K category, which had an elevation gain of about 925m.

Being the shortest ultramarathon I have ever faced, I kept telling myself, "It's only a 50km run", "How hard can it be?" and "What could go wrong?"

Yercaud is a small hill station located in South India at an altitude of 1400m, with coffee estates covering most of the area. The cool weather throughout the year gives the place an abundance of flora unique to the climate. Travelling from Salem to Yercaud pre-race day to collect the bib covered almost a half-marathon with a continuous elevation gain of over 1300m. "Not a bad course to run someday," I thought.

At 4.30 am from Retreat ground, the run began. There were 53 runners in the 50K category. And one of them was Jomy Varghese. We had run together in Malnad, Spice Coast and Vagamon Marathons. It would be good to share a sentence or two with a friendly face during the run. It was surprising to find myself in the lead pack. From what I could make out in the dark, there were three runners ahead of me. The climate was icy with no chilly winds. That was quite a relief. It must have taken an hour to catch up to the lead two runners who happened to be running

together. Later I understood that they were in the 25K category. It seems the 25K and 50K categories started at the same time. It was just before sunrise. The 25K runners had to turn back at a timing mat and I had to move forward. Now the sun was up and peeking between the trees. The coolness in the atmosphere was still there.

Running ultras in Vagamon and Malnad, I am used to seeing course markings a few hundred meters apart. The YHU had such markings at every kilometer or two. Being the lone runner in that stretch of the road, it was worrying if I were on the right course or not. Any mistake now could cost me dearly, for I figured I was somewhere in the top 3. A friendly policeman surveying the runners informed me that I was on the right course and four others ahead of me.

Kilometer 15 to 25 was all downhill. Whatever the terrain may be, downhills have always been my thing. Doing 500 jumping jacks, 100 push-ups, and 200 lunges four days before YHU may have prepared my quads and calves for comfortable long down-hills here. The following 7 km were an ascent. What looked like a participant from the north-eastern part of India, whom I am dearly addressing as 'China Man', made his way past me saying 'Good Running.'

How could he say that? I was walking.

Trying to catch up to China Man with the run-walk method was unsuccessful. Then it was Benil's turn to go past me. I didn't even try to chase him because he looked that good and cheerful on the ups. It did not take much time to lose sight of him too. My dream of finishing in the top 5 was completely smashed. Soon Jomy caught up to me. We may have run together for about 5 km when I began to feel a not-so-funny sensation in my right knee.

"It must be due to the cold climate," I thought.

Soon the tiny sensation turned into a terrible pain. At one point, I almost fell from a fragile feeling in that knee. This was when I knew that it was severe. I was expecting lower back pain plaguing me since my first marathon back in 2017. But this was new. Jomy and I stopped. He advised me to spray the Volini and to shorten my stride length. Jomy was not doing too well either. His calf muscles were on the verge of cramping. Between the previous month's Vagamon 90K and YHU, all Jomy could do was 10km of training. The Volini had zero effect on me because this was not muscular pain. I could feel it inside the knee bone. It had been three years since I had begun running and this knee had been working perfectly fine. But not today. Restarting running after restocking from the aid station was most painful. I had to limp for a few meters before I could overcome the momentary pain. I still used Volini for the Placebo Effect. Maybe imagining it would get better would make it better. There was 20 km more to go.

"Once you hit rock bottom, then the only way is up."

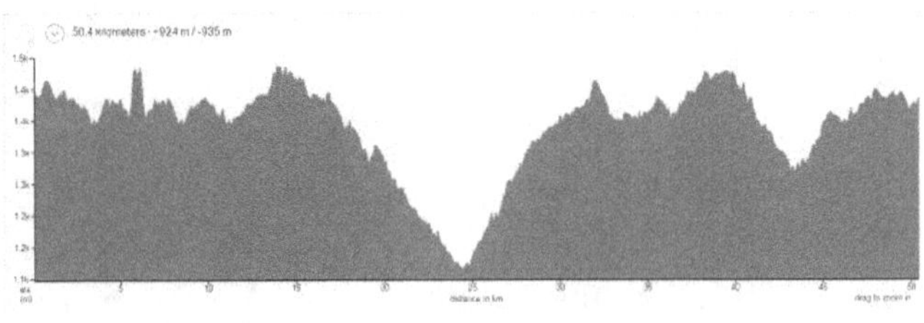

YHU Elevation Profile

I have learned that my body's endurance level during an event looks a lot like the elevation profile of 50K YHU. There is a steady flat portion at the beginning, then comes the low, and next comes the high! It happened to me in 2019 Malnad 80K, it happened during Vagamon 90K in 2020 and YHU 2020 was no exception. These days all my runs are just a mental preparation for the definite disaster to come and overcome it.

I say to myself, "This will go bad and you will also find a way out of it."

The climate was not exactly cold. This was just the way I liked it. I wanted it to be slightly hot. The pain subsided to a level 3. Endurance running brings out emotions onto the surface for some

people. I am one of those people. Especially whenever I come out of pain during events, I become emotional.

"How can you be crying and running uphill at the same time!" I thought.

All the memories of the daily discipline and the hard training flooded my mind. As part of training for YHU, once a week, I would stay back after work to do hill reps on a nearby hill by the name of 'Maniyanthram Mala.' It would be as late as 10 pm after commuting back home.

Soon China Man was back in sight. He was walking uphill. I ran past him and chased down Benil too. A little later, a runner by the name of Yuvaraj was also walking on an ascent. I caught him too. I could not believe that I overtook all those people on the uphill.

How could this be? Was it the climate? The training?

I had no idea. A volunteer at an aid station confirmed that I was in second place. From there on, the tears looked like a waterfall. I imagined what second place would mean to my wife and family. I imagined keeping the second place trophy on the lecture stand before my students. How much it would inspire them to chase their dreams and go beyond their present mind and body.

Dr. Joe Dispenza, a renowned neuroscientist, found that about 1200 'body healing chemical reactions happen in the human body when a person is in a state of total gratitude. I imagined that if I could get any of those reactions to work now, it would be an enormous boost for me. This must be the most emotional I have been during a run. I tried to be gracious and stay in that emotion as long as possible because tears are natural painkillers. Since restarting a run was very excruciating on the knee, there was only one solution.

Do not stop moving. All the nutrition from the remaining aid stations was consumed in that way. "Every marathon is a test", I said at an aid station.

With 5 km to go, the race volunteers informed me that Ganesh Kumar was running in the first place. I tried my best to catch him by running most up-hills. But every stretch of road I came across and every corner I turned, I found it was only me in it.

"Who is this Ganesh, and what the heck is he?" I asked myself.

He is a 43-year-old who has done a few 100 milers and has biked from the west coast to the east coast of USA (3000 miles), Kashmir to Kanyamukari, to name a few. In 2019, he resigned from Intel in the USA to move to Coimbatore in India, where he continues to spend quality time on his bike and his feet.

Two more kilometers remained now. Some of the 12.5K and 25K runners were leaving after completing their run. They were all cheering me on. "Super running!" "Superb!" Not used to hearing such comments, I felt more embarrassed than empowered. Finally, the Retreat ground was ahead of me. A priest happened to be in my path. "Praise be to God" I blurted out. It startled him and he repeated the same. "Yes, praise be to God."

The last 500 meters or so was a trail on the hillside overlooking the city of Salem. By now, my right knee was on its knees, begging me to stop. I kept glancing back to check for runners behind me.

No one came through. The final timing mat was crossed in 5 hours and 42 minutes from the start and in second position. It was my first ever podium finish in a marathon. Yuvaraj completed in 5.43, Benil in 5.45 and Jomy in 5.46.

Me, Ganesh and Yuvaraj

People were coming up to me and shaking my hand when the memento distribution was done. What a fantastic moment it was!

"Why don't you start concentrating on improving your timing?" Dad encouraged me.

The wife was blown away when she heard the news. Savio was equally surprised. Pretty Lil Hearts was surprised. The whole world was surprised!

This is proof that if you want something in life, no one and nothing can stop you. This is proof that if your mind decides, the body will achieve. This is proof that when you are on the right path, magical things will happen. The knee pain remained for two months after YHU 2020 as a reminder of the magic that happened that day.

With Savio John (Poster by Pretty Lil Hearts)

THE PERFECT MARATHON

"O my God!"

"How the heck am I going to run 50km tomorrow morning?"

"I did not plan for this."

It all started a week before the run when my running buddy Rejesh Cyriac compelled me to do the Tuffman 50K Solo Run 2020. It was a virtual event scheduled for the 4th and 5th of July 2020 during the corona-virus pandemic. In my view, a marathon needs to be on the course with the other runners. At least that was what I thought. Anyways, Rejesh is not a person you say no to. So I agreed. The plan was to run along the entire Kochi metro route.

Three days before the event, I started having second thoughts due to a hectic upcoming weekend at a nearby place called Chellanam. So the idea of the 50km was dropped. And I went on with my regular training runs throughout that week.

The night before the event, it was announced on television that Chellanam was under lockdown due to the pandemic.

Great.

It meant that I had to do the Tuffman 50K the next day on a Saturday. The time was now 7 pm. I had to be up the next day by 2 am. After having a banana-peanut butter smoothie, I went to sleep.

Race Day

My home would serve as the aid station. Everything was laid out on the sit-out. The safest place to run was a 3.4 km loop of a road just outside my home.

After having two bananas, the run began at 3.10 am with a headlamp. It was the first time I had ever had any nutrition before a morning run. The headlamp was essential as there was no shortage of snakes like vipers, cobras, kraits and even pythons in my village. After every loop, I made it a point to go home and get some hydration and nutrition.

I decided to run throughout the loop. It was not a decision but an attempt. Somehow the run felt different. It was easier than most days. The breathing felt fine. It was also about to rain.

Soon it did. This was my first rain run during an event. At 35km, my body felt strong enough to keep running a lot more. The most I have run like this was up to 28km at Spice Coast Marathon 2019, beyond which I had to include walking too.

You lose all concept of time when running feels great. Today was one such day. It made me believe that I could run every kilometre in this marathon. It has been my dream ever since I began running.

To run all 42.2kms (apart from stopping at the aid stations).

Finally, that came to happen in 4 hrs and 22 mins. I took the time to stop mid-loop from spending a minute to enjoy what was accomplished. It took me almost three years to achieve this.

Not used to running in aqua shoes that have no cushion, the bottom of my feet started to hurt. The last time I did 50km was back in February during the Yercaud Hills Ultra 50K, after which I got injured and could not run for two months. So after 45km, I decided to walk the rest of the run. Well-wishers out and about doing their business in the morning enquired as to why I was walking.

At 48km, I tried to run again. This led to the quads, adductors and calves on both legs cramping. A triple bonanza!

After giving it one more go, I ran the last kilometre to finish the Tuffman 50K in 5 hrs and 42 mins on a flat course with two bananas and 4 energy gels.

If it weren't for Rejesh, I would have missed knowing that I could have run every kilometer in a full marathon.

Salute!

The following popped into my mind during the run.

"Whenever life hits me, I may bend like a nail but never break."
TUFFMAN 50K SOLO RUN 2020

PUSH-UP WORLD

Unable to run from a minor ankle ligament pull, and after seeing my friend and triathlete Bineesh Thomas post a pic about doing 500 push-ups in the 'Team Learners' WhatsApp group, that motivated me to start doing some pushing up of my own. A year later, Bineesh and Chandu Santhosh became the first people to complete a full triathlon distance of 3.9km swim, 180.2km ride, and 42.2km run inside India.

I started my first step into the 'Push Up' world on a Monday at a rate of 10 push-ups every minute for 10 mins and did that for the whole week. Then, I moved on to 150 push-ups in 15 mins in the next week. Then 200, 250, 300 and so on. Muscular definitions I had never seen before began to appear in the deltoid, triceps, and chest parts.

With Nova

During the 350-a-day week on Sunday, I had a splitting headache from specific issues in the family and from not eating meals at the right time. That left me unable to do the day's workout.

Still, it was my fault. To compensate for the 350 push-ups I missed on Sunday, and instead of doing 400 push-ups during the next week, I did 450.

Then came the 500-a-day week. The previous year, it took 5 hours to complete 500. Now with proper training, I could do it in 50 mins. At that time, I learned about a Physical Education instructor Joby Michael who was from Thrissur. Joby was built like a rock and did a thousand push-ups during the lockdown. It gave me hope that I could do the same.

But conditions were not too favourable on my side. I had taken over 10,000 push-ups in the last seven weeks, and my palms began to hurt. Moreover, this activity was consuming too much time when I did not have the time.

From 500-a-day a week, I jumped to 600 and did that on the first and second day. On the third day, I biked 115kms and did 600 push-ups too. It inspired me to go for 800 on the fourth day. On the fifth day, my left arm and biceps did not feel right after jumping from 600 to 800. So I took a rest.

On day 6 of Week 9, I was on top of the world to know what took me 23 hrs to accomplish last year; I now did it in 100 mins in the perfect form and with a smile on my face.

Some people told me doing too many push-ups would be bad for the joints. But what they should have said was, "Strengthen your joints."

Some people said "അമിത അളവിൽ അമൃതം വിഷമാണ്."

(Even too much of the elixir-of-life is poison.) But how can anyone define "അമിതം?"

(Excess)

Just give a guess which push-up was the hardest one?

It was not the 1000th. It was the first one. The hardest thing is to start.

Remember how I cried the last time I went for 1000? There was none of that on this day. Once you start, the momentum and the right reasons will keep you going.

It took 18,000 push-ups in training to get here. 1000 push-ups in 100 mins CAN'T HURT ME.

Picture taken after the event

CYCLING FOR CHARITY

Aww, man! How can I keep running like this!

The magically appeared ankle ligament pain on the left foot is once again causing me trouble.

It did not bother me much when I ran my fastest marathon in 4 hrs and 15mins in July 2020. But a month later, it's starting to bother me, especially while attempting the 4x4x48.

In the 4x4x48 endurance challenge created by David Goggins, one has to run 4 miles every 4 hours for 48 hours. That's 77kms in two days. Four miles is just a fun run for the average runner. But to keep doing that at an interval of 4 hours while managing your rest, nutrition, and daily chores is no easy task. I chose 8 pm, 12 am, 4 am, 8 am, 12 pm, and 4 pm. The ideal 6-8 hour beauty sleep requirement goes out the window when you do this. Since I chose my village roads as the running route, I also dealt with people staring at me in utter confusion.

Midnight run

This 4x4x48 is a workout for gaining an extra ounce of mental strength than whatever you had before. It toughens you up. It is a way of saying to the onlookers:

"I will do whatever I want, whenever I want and however I want."

We let ourselves be influenced so much by others that it has paralyzed us to attempt anything new in our lives. What will they think? What will people say? Won't they call me crazy? At a young age, we need to realize that the probability of people coming to our rescue in times of need is very low. If we develop the ability to come out of those moments when we feel we are sinking, life will have a whole new meaning. Only then will we discover the tools to help ourselves. This 4x4x48 is the perfect tool to thicken our skin.

To complete this challenge for the first time in 2020 during the lockdown was a considerable achievement.

Since then, the ankle pain has gotten worse. Any distance above 5km was painful. The first physiotherapist I consulted used ultrasound frequency treatment and infra-red heat treatment over the problematic area. That lessened the pain but failed to remove it for good. Then I consulted the acupuncturist who had cured the Cuboid Syndrome I had a year before. After a ten-day consultation, the pain was gone entirely. He also advised me to strengthen the ankles, which I failed to follow up. Needless to say, that ankle pain resurfaced at the next run.

I was devastated.

Two doctors in two different areas of expertise could not cure me.

"What do I do next?" I asked myself. Extended periods of rest did not help either.

It was at this time that I decided to get on the bike.

There was a 5000 rupee single-speed bike I used for the last seven years to commute to the bus stop.

It would take anywhere from six to seven hours to cover a distance of 100kms on this bike.

The next question I asked was, "What would a 24-hour ride on a gearless bike look like?" If I'm going to ride this long, then why not put it into good use?

That was how the concept of cycling for charity came into being. The idea was to go from Cochin to Calicut beach and back without sleeping anywhere in between. That meant covering a distance of 320km along the NH 17 highway via Guruvayoor. This route had minimal elevation compared to NH 47. The proposed date for the event was on December 12th 2020, and it would once again be for Emmanuel Children's Home.

Thomas Brother and his wife were excited at the idea. One of their girls even drew a picture of me on a bike. My history of official and unofficial endurance events and photos of the previous fundraiser were all used for the online promotion of the event. WhatsApp and Facebook were used for publicity. Instagram was an alien tech to me at the time. This time I sought the support of the alumni of the college too.

There was a plan to have my wife and brother follow me in the car. But that got dropped in the weeks leading to it. This was where Mr. Sajeesh G. Nair came to my rescue. Though the trip was meant to be a solo one, Sajeesh offered to ride with me along the entire route. The offer came just the day before the event. Of course, I said yes.

December 12th 2020, before sunrise:

The ride began from St. Joseph Church ground at Varapuzha at 4 in the morning. My family was there to see me off. Sajeesh joined me from Paravoor 10kms en route. There was still an hour left for the first light of the day. My student and cyclist, Dhon Paul, had the heart to lend me his front and rear lamps to navigate in the dark.

The aim was to make it to Calicut Beach, 160kms away before

sunset, and then turn back. The ride up to Guruvayoor felt fine and smooth. The early morning coolness and wide roads kept our spirits high. Stopping at a restaurant for dosa and chutney, the establishment owner enquired us if we were making the trip for any reason in particular. Sajeesh Bhai was always the one to answer questions like these while I more or less stayed silent and smiled. Now and then, I took photographs of the route and shared them online. Where pictures failed to describe certain events, I used voice messages to convey the story. It kept everyone interested as a fair idea was given of all the things that happened during those two days.

2014 Btwin single speed bike

In 6 hours, we made it through Ponnani. 100 km had been crossed at a speed of 16 km/hr. After Ponnani, there was a left turn to Chamravattom Bridge. But we missed it. Riding at noon with no tree cover along an 11 km stretch of straight road, I forgot to check the map. But it was ok. The alternative route took 11 extra kilometres through Kuttippuram along the Bharathapuzha riverside through Thirunavaya. Soon we reached BP Angadi and were back on track. Then due to a particular turn of events, a surprise was awaiting us at Parappanangadi.

Sajeesh Bhai's stomach had been troubling him for a while, and we hadn't had lunch either. So, we stopped at a restaurant at Parappanangadi. A group of friendly locals at the place had a chitchat with us. What they asked us next startled us.

One of them wearing a lungi, asked, "Would you mind giving us a bite?" "A what?" I blurted out.

"Yes, a sound bite for an interview," he continued and flashed his news-reporter ID card.

The card showed Malabar News Reporter. That was how Sajeesh Bhai and I got my first ever video channel interview. They also took a variety of moving video shots with us on our bikes. Half an hour later, they were done with the shoot, and we were on our way to Calicut Beach.

It was almost sunset and we had made it into Calicut city. My friend Abdul Gafoor was kind enough to set me up a service check for our bikes at Calicut Stadium Junction at Cafe Werkstatt. Friends from the running club Royal Runners Calicut (RRC), Abraham and Arun, waited for our arrival there. Ever since the ride had started, there was a noise every time my pedal made one full rotation. The people at Werkstatt found out that the bottom bracket was faulty and had to be replaced. Luckily, the correct spare was available and owing to the charity ride, it was fixed free of labour charge. Sajeesh Bhai had his bike seat set. While all this was being done, we were treated with oranges. Jees Mathew, a student of my college living nearby, bought us watermelons.

After riding for 14 hours, we reached Calicut at 6 in the evening. A picture of Sajessh Bhai and me was taken at the beach for social media. After calling home, we were on our way back. During the return journey, we decided it was better we used the Beach road to Parappanangadi. Unlike the Theeradesha Road, this was the narrow strip of the road right next to the sea. It was slightly bumpy and slower but had very little traffic. We also got to interact with the locals here. It was the last day of the Panchayath election campaign and there were lots of people still hanging around on this route. The yellow cycling top and the flashing headlights made sure that we caught everyone's attention. Many times out of curiosity, people would stop us to ask what we were doing around these parts at this time of the night. At first, they would call us crazy. But when they were told that it was for charity, they appreciated us. We also got to have a conversation with a guy on his Lambi scooter for a couple of minutes as we kept riding. After getting to know the details of the ride, he removed his helmet to show the long hair he had been sporting. He was a 'Hair Donation Club' member, and the donations were for cancer patients at Amala Hospital in Thrissur.

"Wow! That seemed so much cooler than what we were doing." I thought.

Almost all of the people who talked to us along the Beach Road asked us if we had had any supper or anything to drink. They even invited us into their homes for a meal or a tea break. The invitations came up to 11 in the night. But since the clock was ticking, we politely declined every offer received.

Soon we reached what seemed to be the end of the beach road and entered a 'coconut forest'. The place was utterly dark. We had to get down on foot and walk our way through it. It only cost us a few minutes.

December 13th 2020, 2 am:

I am not a night person. On any given day, I have a tough time staying awake past 10 pm. So you can imagine how difficult it was to keep my eyes open at this time of the night. I must have nearly fallen off the bike a dozen times mid-ride. The guardian angels on both sides must have kept me on balance. Trying to stay awake by singing out loud and riding fast did not do any good. I had hallucinations of seeing road bumps and large stones in the middle of the road. These experiences were shared on social media. The Director of Emmanuel Children's Home, Thomas Brother, sent me a voice message of him praying to get us back safe and sound. Sajeesh Bhai, on the other hand, seemed to be doing well. The only issue he had been having was saddle soreness. Soon we were back on the NH 17 highway. At 4 am, we decided to get a power nap in front of a shop beside the road.

8 minutes.

That was the only sleep we got. I woke up to find my co-rider snoring at the top of his voice. The power nap did not do much good. Sleep finally wore off when the first light of the day appeared. Sunlight increases your blood glucose levels and keeps you active. Now I believe it.

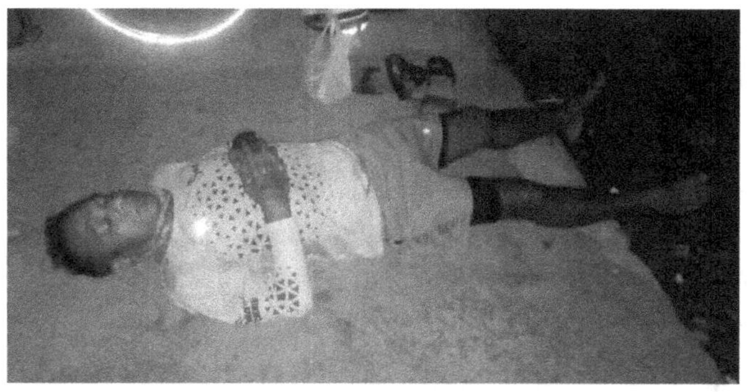

Just about to wake up Sajeesh after an 8-minute sleep

By now, the effects of the long journey were finally starting to get to us. It was increasingly difficult to ride continuously, even for 30 minutes. We were not in the mood to have any breakfast and wanted to get to the comfort of our homes without wasting much time. Noontime was fast approaching.

It was at this time, another friend Prasad Kanakasseri from RRC, texted me.

"സാമൂതിരിയുടെ പെരുമയേന്തുന്ന കോഴിക്കോടിന്റ മണൽ തരികളെപ്പോലും പുളകം കൊള്ളിച്ചുകൊണ്ട് കടന്നുപോയ രണ്ട് യോദ്ധാക്കളിതാ.."

"ഭൂമിയിലെ മാലോകർക്ക് പിടിച്ചുകെട്ടാനാവാത്ത യാഗാശ്വങ്ങളെപ്പോലെ, പടക്കോപ്പുകളേന്തി പടപൊരുതാനുറച്ച പടയാളികളെ പ്പോലെ, അവരിതാ മുന്നേറിക്കൊണ്ടിരിയ്ക്കുന്നു.."

"തൃശ്ശിവപ്പേരൂരിന്റെ നഗരവീഥികളെ കാൽക്കീഴിലാക്കി കടന്നുപോയ.." "ഏതാനും നാഴികകൾ ക്കൂടി പിന്നിടുമ്പോൾ എറണാകുളത്തപ്പന്റെ മണ്ണിൽ ചവിട്ടി വിജയക്കൊടി പ്പാറിയ്ക്കാൻ പോകുന്ന ധീര യോദ്ധാക്കളെ നിങ്ങൾക്ക് ലോകത്തിന്റെ നമോവാകം."

Translation:

"Here are two warriors who passed through the dunes of Calicut, the pride of the Zamorin. They are advancing, like sacrificial horses that the world can not hold back, like soldiers ready to fight with their weapons and have passed through the city streets of Thrissivaperoor. A few hours later, you will be greeted by the brave warriors who will set foot on the soil of Ernakulam and hoist the victory flag."

By 10 am, we reached Paravoor Signal Junction. It was where Sajeesh Bhai had to take a turn to get to his home. One last selfie was taken here. This photo later made its way into the article in the Malayala Manorama newspaper.

After being on the road for 31 hours and covering a distance of 330 km, the charity ride finally came to an end on Sunday at 11 am right where it had started. My family and in-laws were waiting with placards for my arrival.

Rs. 1,73,830 was raised by the combined efforts of friends, family, students and alumni.

When the details of the event were published in the newspaper, I even got a call from 93.5 Red FM Station at Kakkanad. It was RJ Nitha asking for an interview. Cycling for charity was a concept she wanted to explore.

With RJ Nitha

Just look at all the things that magically happened because I could not run for a while. Look at all the blessings that came on the way.

It is not magic.

What seems magical to others is hard work and perseverance to the achiever. Only that person knows the truth behind the magic. Like you cannot explain magic, you cannot explain all the effort it took to put thoughts into action. Everything that had ever happened in your life was to bring you to this precise moment. Good things can arise from the bad.

All it takes is a little time, effort, and companionship with people like Sajeesh Bhai.

#Gearless & Fearless

HUNDRED MILE HEROES

Two words.

The first one is 'dream.' It is defined as follows:

'a series of thoughts, images, and sensations occurring in a person's mind during sleep.' The second word is 'great.' My definition is 'achieving a little more than yesterday.'

Some dream with their eyes open. They spend every waking moment in the pursuit of greatness.

Then some fall into the category of "just do it." These are the people who take a blind leap of faith just because they know that the outcome will be nothing short of greatness. This is the story of ten runners who signed up for the 2020 Konkan 100 miler virtual event and shocked the entire running community in Kerala. Under the able guidance of veteran marathoner Paul Padinjekkara, this was the designated course to be adopted:

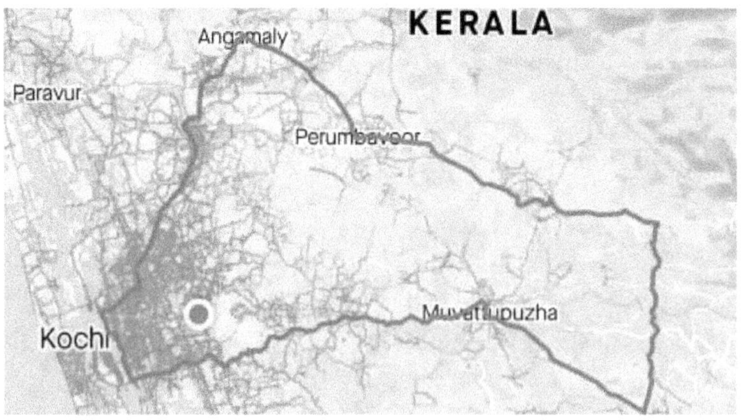

Route Map

With five other supporting runners, the run began in high spirits on January 2nd at 4 am. To the average man, all this celebration at the starting line would seem confusing. Why would anyone seem so happy to keep moving on foot for a hundred and sixty kilometres? The more you try to explain it, the more it loses its value. I have always felt that the best answers are those that you discover by yourself.

There were two support cars, one exclusively for the lead runner and one for all the others. The vehicles contained adequate nutrition and hydration.

The lead runner in the discussion here is Rejesh Cyriac. Rejesh is an ultramarathoner who competes at podium level. He is also one of the core members of the 'Team Learners' WhatsApp group. Later, he started a natural weight loss group that did not involve any exercise or fasting, which changed the lives of a lot of people. It was only a month before the event that he was struck down with Covid - 19. A month before this event, he ran a full marathon, not knowing he had caught the Covid-19 infection.

The support car at the back would halt every 5 km to provide adequate nutrition and water. I was on my gearless bike and had the job of supplying water between those 5 km points. There was one other person on cycle support. He was Akhil S Pai. But his bike had a gear malfunction just after the run began. So the bike had to be kept for safe-keeping at a nearby friend's home, and he used another one from a runner's home at Muvattupuzha. Both of us would stock up on water from the car and go back and forth to hydrate all those in need.

The oldest runner in the pack was Paul Padinjekkara. a.k.a Panther Paul. Even at the ripe old age of 67, he puts in 100k weeks. For his 65th birthday, he did 65 miles. He is also the only person who has done a 100 miler before. People call him 'The Sachin Tendulkar of Running'.

"If Paulettan can do it, then we can do it."

This was the adopted mentality by the other runners.

It was all smiles and joy at the beginning. Under the cover of darkness, the runners made their way till Kolenchery. By 8 am, we reached Muvattupuzha. 30kms had been covered in the coolness of the morning weather.

Between Saturday 4 pm and Sunday 8 am, I had to go to the toilet seven times from eating papaya on Saturday that went bad.

But it's ok.

Five other runners ran almost a third of the distance with the 100 milers to show their solidarity. Spreading the message of preserving nature and promoting exercise was the secondary motive of the Konkan virtual run. Mr. Pradeepkumar Menon (age 50) made sure he talked about both those subjects on Facebook Live whenever he stopped beside the car and en route. This was a massive risk for him. Energy management is of prime importance during endurance activity, and every time you talk, your body takes a bite into your energy storage. But it had to be done. The message of preserving Mother Nature had to be spread.

The sun was right above our heads. Most of the runners were starting to feel the intensity of the run. This was also the time of the day, and I was the busiest. I only had an 800ml bottle to supply water in between those 5 km mobile aid stations. So the water ran out quickly. Multiple trips to the car were made to restock the water.

From kilometre 40, another participant Abdul Gafoor was experiencing issues on his left knee. It was IT band syndrome. After walking a few more kilometres with a walking stick made out of a tree branch, he made the right decision to quit at the 45th kilometre and got into the support car. This was his first attempt at doing an ultramarathon. At the 48km point, the support runners bid goodbye. They had done their part to motivate the others. The stretch of road to Oonnukal had some elevation but also a good amount of tree shade.

Be it sun or shade; there was one runner called Sajeesh Nair who ran topless and barefoot till the 48km point. He is also a triathlete. While most runners were using UV protection tops, Sajeesh was quite happy running half-naked. All the time, he kept saying that he was solar-powered.

At Oonnukal, all of us enjoyed hot kanji (porridge) from a hotel. Mr. Ben Thomas, a.k.a Ben Johnson, had come from his home at Adimali to cheer up the runners.

The lead runner, Rejesh was starting to feel the burden by now. He committed a grave error on his part by deciding to sleep off for 45 minutes inside his support car. That cooled down his legs and made them stiff. Later, he fell hard after tripping on a road stone and splitting a toenail. That was his signal to end the race. He quit at kilometre 75.

By 5 pm, everyone crossed Oonnukal. Paulettan began the black coffee therapy to keep the running spirit alive. So did the others. Jithin Paul and Xavier Peter were starting to spend minimal time at hydration points.

The route from Kothamangalam to Perumbavoor had the most traffic and the least streetlights. All the running was done on the side of the road against the traffic. This kept running to a minimum in this portion of the race. Everyone consumed their last sit-down meal of the event from Odakkali. The energy the runners had was admirably high, but it was draining fast. My legs were also starting to hurt. I only had three hours of sleep before I had left home.

"If this was what I was feeling, what must the runners be going through?" I thought.

Prasannan was one of the two runners from Kottayam Running Club. Prasannan had done over 100,000 feet of elevation gain in 2020. He always talked less and ran more. Renju Jacob was the second person. He was even more silent than Prasannan. He was an ultra-silent ultra runner.

At Perumbavoor, Ashramam Joggers surprised all of us with their warm reception mid-race. They gave us hot coffee and a lot of encouragement. After all, it was the first hundred-miler run Kerala had seen.

It had been over 18 hours, and almost all the runners were exhausted. All except one.

Jose Ellickal, a.k.a Josettan, is a health insurance agent from the hilly regions of Wayanad. He was a professional tug of war athlete. Before the hundred-mile event, it had been only six months since he got into running. He immediately started running at lightning speeds of 4 minutes per km for half marathons and above. He had done a full marathon only once, and that was a sub-3-hour run. But all of that was done on a dirt track and not on the road. Everyone was interested to know what would be the outcome of his run today.

From Perumbavoor, when the roads were wide enough to run freely again, I felt that he was still in the mood to pick up his pace. Since it was past midnight and the climate was favourable, I was not needed to stay with the runners at the back end. So I urged Josettan to run till the next spot where the support car was parked. And he would do it comfortably in one or two continuous runs at a pace not slower than 5.30 per km. This performance at 90 km into the run was outstanding! He did that up to the 160th kilometer.

After reaching the support car well in advance of the other runners, Josettan would remove his shoes, sit on the pavement and get some stretching done. It was also a chance to glimpse what was going through his mind during the event, his training philosophy and aspirations.

Once, he ran a sub-3 marathon on a dirt ground with a few mouthfuls of salt lime water. Amazed at such a feat, I asked him how come he did not 'hit the wall' like the rest of us. A typical human being has about 2000 kcal stored in the body. 'Hitting the wall' is a common phrase which runners use to indicate the condition where they have run out of stored energy during a run. Usually, running comes to a dead stop at this point.

"Is it? I haven't heard about it. Therefore, it never affects me." replied Josettan.

What the heck did I hear! I was stunned.

Apparently, since Josettan does not believe in science, it does not affect him.

Another funny thing about his nutrition is that, unlike most runners, he ate a bucket load of rice on race morning. For lunch, he had rice water. He is the only person I have seen with veins bulging out of his leg. It looked like roots exposed above the soil.

Josettan would joke that a cut-off limit of 30 hours is not needed for this event. The best way to finish a 100 miler is to run 50km in the morning on the ground. Go home. Eat plenty. Sleep well. Wake up in the evening. Do another 50km. Then do 60km the next morning. Hundred-miler done!

It is why we call him 'The Wayanadan Beast.'

At 3.30 am on day 2, we were at Angamaly. Beyond this point, I could not support the runners as I had to go to work. It was Monday. After wishing them all the best for successful completion, I bid them goodbye and rode home. As soon as I was out of the company of the others, sleep hit me like a rock. Staying balanced on my bike almost seemed impossible. Luckily, there was a coffee shop open, and I had black coffee. I nearly fell face-first into the coffee cup as I was cooling it. After having a couple of Little Hearts biscuits, the sleepiness went away, and I got back on the bike. I was also on the lookout for the two runners in the lead.

They were Xavier Peter and Jithin Paul.

Xavier is a podium-level runner with a down-to-earth attitude. I still remember the post-run speech he made at the reception given by Royal Runners Calicut to these 100 milers later on.

"Since childhood, all I ever dreamt of was sports, sports and only sports." That was Xavier Peter.

The hundred-miler run was his return to the spotlight after being plagued by numerous injuries for the past two years. But he had been having trouble with his knees today.

Jithin was the youngest runner in the group. Being the highly ambitious guy he already was, he (as well as Xavier) wanted to complete the run in less than 30 hours. After the 75th kilometer, they left the aid of the support car and went on their own.

Jithin ended up crossing the finish line at Tripunithura in 28 hours 40 minutes taking first place. Xavier came in second, a few minutes behind Jithin.

Josettan felt strong enough to complete the event in time, and with the hydration support offered by Mevin Pius, who was on his bike, Josettan made it in 29 hours and 30 minutes. Mevin Pius is a 100km per day cyclist who came from Thrissur to support the event. He arrived after my departure.

Sajeesh Nair had to quit after 125 kilometers, due to a football injury he had a few weeks earlier. With Panther Paul pulling the ropes, Pradeep, Prasannan, and Renju finished the event in about 34 hours. It was a dream come true for them.

This is the story of how a small group of runners from the southernmost part of India took on the 100-mile road challenge and ended up having the experience of a lifetime. Their efforts on that day went on to inspire many more runners to push their limits and unlock their minds.

THE GOLDEN DAYS

The college days were the best, weren't they? Those days will never come back. After graduating from college, everyone feels that those were the golden days. I used to believe that too.

When I was in school, I thought those were the best days of my life. When I got to college, I thought they were the best. When I had just become a teacher, those were the best days. But after doing a bunch of endurance events in 2019, I thought that would be my best year. Every year will keep staying golden as long as you keep polishing it with gold.

But gold does not come cheap. You have to make an effort to dig it out of the earth.

Often we come across people who put in a tremendous amount of work to get what they want in life. Imagine the guy who went to the gym to 'get the girl' or the ladies that stayed lean to 'get the guy'. Then one fine day, they finally get what they want. Now what? What are the new reasons to keep doing the things that made them better? If the answer is none, then the chances are that they had the wrong mentality in the first place.

There is only one person for who you should be doing anything. It is you. Do it for you.

Do not do it for your parents. Do not do it for your husband or wife. Do not even do it for God. Your mind is the only thing that will always be with you. Based on your actions, you hold conversations with yourself more than with anyone else. Finish those conversations in a way that your inner voice is proud of your efforts done today and not with what you had done years before.

That heavenly feeling of crossing the finishing line of a 100-mile run or passing a job interview, or getting the girl of your dreams they do not last. Aren't all these yesterday's news?

In the world of newsprint, yesterday's news has pretty much no value today. The reader wants to know what has happened today. At the end of the day, the feeling of content will not be from all

the productive things that happened yesterday. It comes from all the essential things you did today. This is why what you do every day matters. Be rooted in the present.

In 2019, I did 1000 push-ups in a day for the first time. Getting that done felt great. A couple of months later, I started asking myself, "Do I want to be someone that did a thousand push-ups just once in the past, or do I want to be someone that does a thousand push-ups?" I chose the second part. But that also meant I had to do the work to stay in my best form every day. I had to keep myself focussed and empowered.

1000 push-ups in 24 hours showed the way to do 1000 push-ups in 100 mins in 2020. In 2021, I began to think about what it would look like if push-ups were done for 24 hours without sleeping. That was how I discovered 3000 push-ups could be done in 24 hours in February of 2021.

Poster for the 24 Hour Max Push Up

The most surprising thing was that there was no muscle pain, joint pain, or uneasiness of any kind the next day.

"How the heck is that possible?" I thought. I had pushed my body to its limit, and the days after that felt as though nothing had happened. It is with things like this that life surprises you. You do something to get the desired outcome. But it is the unexpected bonus that comes along with the work that makes it worthwhile.

Soon after, I began to think, "Who cares if you did all those push-ups?"

If I could include like-minded people to do some push-ups of their own, then I could take the event to the next level. That was how in May of 2021, the idea for a group event came up.

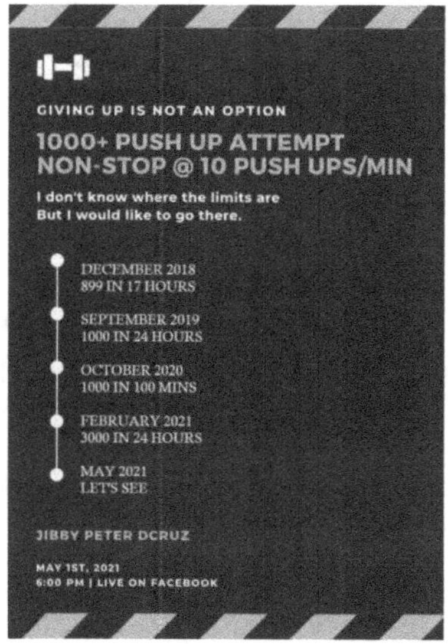

Poster for me

For the participation of others

I did 1270 push-ups in 127 mins. But the exciting part was that eight others from my Team Learners Whatsapp group joined in the event, and they too found out their maximum. Another person, an ultra runner Yamini Kothari residing in Mumbai, took 200 knee push-ups. But it was 375 push-ups from Hrishi Venkitesh and 540 knee push-ups from Maria Sabu that blew my mind. They were engineering students that I had been teaching at the time.

To some runners, completing a 100 miler is the pinnacle of endurance sports. If that was what they believed, then they should have quit running the very next day. But people like them still keep pushing themselves with other challenges.

Just because you nearly drowned in the past does not mean you have to stay afraid of the water. We are nothing but a collection of our past experiences. The only way to change an old or a bad experience is to make a new one in the present. Stop recalling your tragic past. Stop saying things that make you weak. Whatever you say will become your immediate reality.

Do you have a feeling that you are nowhere in life?

In spirituality, there is an understanding that the time is now and the place is here.

All you have is NOW. The present moment is as real as it gets. Try to reset whatever has happened earlier and start fresh today.

All the good, bad, and ugly things that have happened in the past have led you to this exact moment. The whole of the universe has worked very hard to get you HERE.

"Yesterday is history. Tomorrow is a mystery. But today is a gift. That is why it is called the present."

Master Oogway
(From the animation movie Kungfu Panda)

So make the 'now' and 'here' your launching point to take off and never look back.

EFFORT

There is a word that is more important than God. It is called effort. Ask God not with your words but with your actions. Effort matters.

How much effort you put into a situation will make the outcome that much sweeter. Enlightenment does not come from simply sitting under a banyan tree. Enlightenment comes from sitting under a banyan tree after one has done all the hard work.

Meet Prem G Menon. He got into the Indian Navy at the age of 17 as an apprentice and retired as Master Chief Petty Officer twenty years later. His dream was to run from his workplace at Cochin to his home at Athirapally, which was 70 km away. The most suitable day he could find was on the last day of his service. The main intention of the run was to show that drugs and drinks are not the only solutions to setbacks in life. He wanted to express that one can rely on the strength of mind too. But three kilometers from the start, he twisted his ankle. Even with that, he went on to complete the whole thing in 13 hours, thanks to people like Ram Jat, who kept pushing him all the way.

What must have gone through his mind before he made that decision to keep running?

Physical injuries will heal. Pain is temporary. But if you quit, failure is permanent. The pain of not taking a chance will chase you as long as you are alive. It took him the last day of his work to become an actual hero. The world needs more people like Prem G Menon.

Guess what Ram Jat did a year later?

Ram Jat and Sanjay Kumar, two other Indian Navy officers, set a Guinness World Record for running from Kanyakumari to Kashmir. That's 4431 km in 56 days.

It proves that it is never too late for anything and anyone to find their greatness. Greatness is not doing what others cannot do. Greatness is doing something more than whatever you did the previous day.

You are the key. What use is a key if it is driven into a lock and just kept like that? A key works only when it turns.

Just like a key, unless and until we make a whole new turn, nothing will change. We will remain stuck with the same mindset that we used to have.

There were plenty of days when I wanted to sleep in and not do my workouts. Will that be comfortable?

Yes.

But will it do me any good? No.

On a typical weekday, I get anywhere from five and half hours to six hours of sleep. There were plenty of nights where I could not get a sound sleep. I would wake up the next day and search for excuses not to go for a run. I would continue to find reasons while running and even more reasons after the run. But still, it had to be done.

I am now at a point in life where I can boldly say that every effort I took has yielded results. Sometimes you have to override all feelings of comfort to achieve whatever you want in life. These achievements may not come today. They may not even show up in a year. But they will come if you keep striving. Just wait for it. The decision to pick up dumbbells from the age of twelve sowed the seeds of every physical activity I do today.

'Effort' has another friend called 'obstacle.' They both walk hand in hand. Just because you decided to put in the effort does not mean that everything will look like a clear-cut path now. Like a fast-moving car, the faster it goes, the more forces act on it to slow it down. That's just how the universe works. I have had many physical injuries over the years since I picked up running. One of them was Cuboid Syndrome. It is caused when the cuboid bone in the foot moves out of alignment. It is most often the result of injury or trauma to the joint and ligaments surrounding the small tarsal bone. When nothing else worked, it was the acupuncture treatment at the hands of the very versatile Joy Thakarappillil that removed my pain for once and for all. Getting your fingers pricked with 25 needles for ten days is something everyone should experience. Other than acupressure and acupuncture, Joy Thakarappillil has extensive knowledge of reflexology, seed therapy, leaf therapy, colour therapy, cupping therapy, auricular therapy, quantum therapy, magnet therapy, touch healing therapy, angel therapy, crystal healing therapy, counseling course, and all things under the sun. It was he who introduced me to the world of meta-physical right before my eyes. Then there was a troublesome ankle ligament pain that put me out of running for six months until I found the right doctor. It was the proper diagnosis from Dr. Ajeesh T Alex at Actymed Center for Orthopaedics and Sports Medicine that put me back on track. I would hold my breath when the doctor kept poking my calf muscle with a 10-cm needle as part of the dry needling technique.

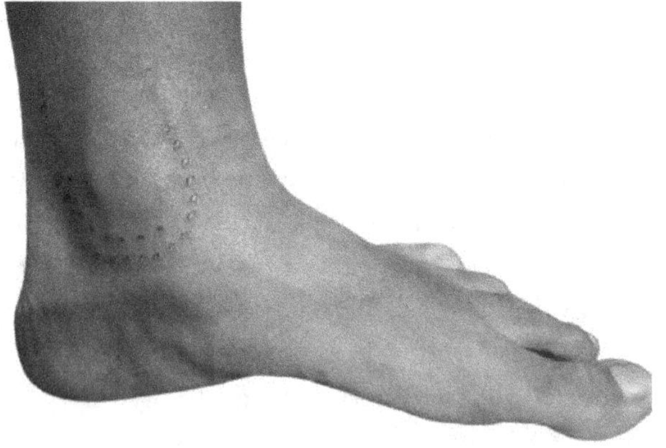

Agnikarma - an ancient Ayurvedic therapy

If pain were something to be avoided, then most of us would not have been born. Our mothers knew that. No mother quits halfway through the pregnancy because of the discomfort she has to put up. She knows that a day will come when her suffering will end with the successful delivery of her beautiful baby.

And why does it matter if it is a workday, holiday, Sunday, or a Monday? These are concepts that we have made up in our minds. Life does not care what day it is. There is the time you get from sunrise to sunset, and that is all. Use it or lose it. There is no guarantee that you may live to see another light.

How good is your reason to do the things you want to do? The right reason will press all the buttons in you to activate the mind. Because my wife and I were blessed with our daughter on our third attempt, for her third birthday I did 300 push-ups with a 5kg weighted vest to celebrate it my way. Not satisfied with that, 1000 lunges were also done in 11 hours the next day.

What is the point in saying 'Good morning'? Make it a good morning. Meditate, stretch, walk, run, bike, swim, write, move. Do anything and win the battle of the morning. If you win the day's battle by attempting something worthwhile, there is a good chance you will win the war of life too. Great experiences await you once you overcome yourself. The real enemy is not on the outside but on the inside. Doubt, fear and procrastination are the things that are holding you back.

A month after the Calicut ride fundraiser, the contributions donated were stuck at Rs. 96,000. I was expecting a bit more because 96,000 was less than what the Solo Sun Run pulled in the previous year. That upset me. It felt as though a journey of 300kms in 31 hours on a gearless bike was not worthy of their attention.

> *"If there is no enemy within, the enemy outside us can do no harm."*
>
> *-An African Proverb*

So I announced through social media that if the funds crossed a hundred thousand rupees, I would do an open-water swim for a distance of 1km at Aluva Manappuram. Soon after, the donations went beyond one lakh rupees. At the time, I was learning the freestyle swimming technique. For an average freestyle swimmer, it takes about 20 minutes to complete a kilometer. But because I had not perfected my breathing technique while doing the freestyle, it took me an hour and 45 minutes to do the same distance.

When you start to empower your mind even when you have no power left, that is when the miracles start happening. Like when my knee recovered during the beach run at Cherai and during Malayattoor climbs, these miracles will seem like a mystery. Sometimes I feel our only purpose in life is to pass the energy to the next person. Tomorrow when you are gone, let there be someone who got infected with a part of your energy. Nobody wants to die, right? This is how you(r energy) live forever.

Life is tough.

But if you make a little more effort, it can get a lot better.

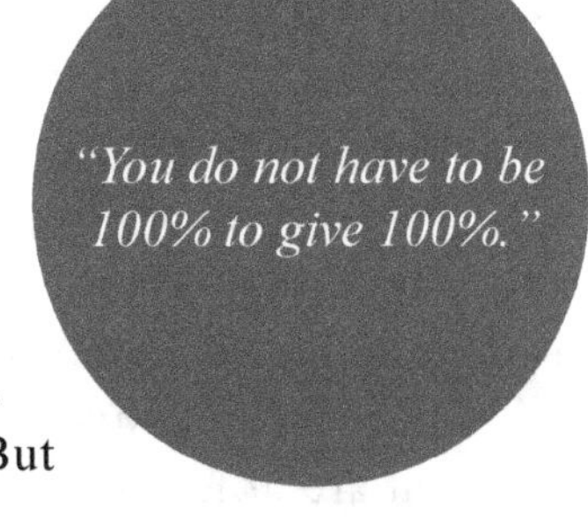

Biking over 300km in 31 hours was already hard on me. Using that as a fundraiser for charity is more effort. But that made all the difference.

Picture of a battery ad taken during the Calicut ride

WHAT ARE YOU WAITING FOR?

We eat, we sleep, and we wake up.

We wake up with the hope that someone or something will change our lives that day. Long back, we had needs. Now they are replaced by wants. Unable to acquire these wants, we conclude that life is ordinary, predictable, or just not worth living at all.

Albert Einstein once said, "Only a life lived for others is a life worthwhile."

I think the truth does not get any better than that. We live lives trying to attain happiness or in the pursuit of happiness, as some may call it. Yet most have a hard time finding it. My question is, why not get happiness simply by giving it? If you want something, you must give it first. How else can it come back to you? Like the circle of life, this keeps going round and round. The more you give, the more you receive. From the time you are born, it has never been about you. Nobody cares what you do for yourself. Instead, it is all about what you can do for others.

We have it in us to be extraordinary. It is up to us to decide whether to wait for the world to keep giving us things or give back to the world without making it wait for us. Our world is not perfect. But every little act of generosity is one step closer to

" It is more blessed to give than to receive."

- Acts of the Apostles, chapter 20 verse 35.

making the world a perfect one. Of course, we can always sympathize with their sorry state or comfort them with words as high as mountains. We might even keep thinking about their despair for a while or even lose one night's sleep over it. But thinking without acting is in itself a thought wasted. The fact is that it does not make their condition any better.

The reality is that action speaks louder than words and worthless sympathies. The true wealth is not measured by the space his money occupies or by the number of people pointed under his finger but by the blessings he gets from the lips of the rest.

So, what is an act of generosity? It is making someone's life better, even if it is least noticeable. True happiness does not come from what you do for yourself. It comes from what you do for others. A good action creates a good memory. Good memories are the fuel to life. So make sure you create enough fuel to last a lifetime.

Don't be a life looking for inspiration. Be an inspiration looking to give life. Life is waiting for you to do something.

What are you waiting for?

THE LAST CHAPTER

Only through getting outside our comfort zone can we achieve our greatness. There is no doubt that running is suffering. There is no enjoyment in being out of breath, sweaty, tired, and sore while running. But that only lasts till the end of the run. What I am trying to say is that pain is only temporary. Moving through life is like getting to the finishing line of a marathon. Now you have become a little stronger. You have become a 'new you.' This world is not going to get easier to live in. Poor people will have 'poor-people problems.' Rich people will have 'rich-people problems.' Famous people will have 'famous-people problems.' Ordinary people will have 'ordinary-people problems.' When life guarantees problems and suffering, why aren't enough people getting ready for it? Even though the finishing line for life is not clearly defined, I would like to think of it as whatever goal you set out for the day. If you achieved the day's goal, then you have crossed the day's finishing line.

But guess what? There is another race to be run the next day with another finishing line waiting for you. It goes on and on and on. There is no end. Accept it and immerse yourself in it. Challenges keep life engaging and interesting.

Life has an annoying habit of placing mountains before you. Now let me rephrase that.

Life has an interesting habit of gifting mountains to you. Climbing mountains is sweaty and hard. But every mountain climbed is a challenge you overcame. You did it. You found the strength to do it. Now, you are no longer the 'old you.' The 'old you' took a step back when you saw that mountain rise before you. But once you overcome that terrifying mountain, it does not feel so scary anymore. A mountain feels like a long-lost friend who helped you overcome fear. It will keep you coming back for another climb. Today, I have convinced myself that if an activity, be it a run or ride or workout, does not take at least 24 hours, it does not classify as an endurance

event. You grow mentally only if you keep redefining the standards that you have set for yourself. There is no other way.

All the ups and downs you have read in this book had to happen. Those incidents define me. In the same way, there is a reason why the incidents in your life have happened to you. The reasons may not be evident initially, but they will make sense later on so that your mindset can expand and grow. The mind, once expanded, can never return to its original dimension. You can never unlearn an idea.

How do you think I got into charity work in the first place? It was my dad, Peter Simon D'cruz, who first inspired me. His act of deciding to marry my mother, Jean Peter, from an orphanage opened my eyes to volunteer for the National Service Scheme (NSS) unit in my college. And guess what came out of that service? The NSS unit, which had 100 student volunteers, was able to conduct government hospital equipment restoration works, blood donation camps, visit orphanages and nursing homes, provide weekly lunch packets to destitute homes, perform street plays on socially relevant issues and do other services in the community. And when I got out of the service in NSS, I took that energy and applied it to raise money for charity through running, biking and swimming. In 2021 after becoming a core committee member of Amradham, I began to do fundraisers for that too. Amradham is an initiative started by the NGO Pretty Lil Hearts to provide free cab services and nutrition to underprivileged pregnant women near Chennai. The first fundraising event for the same was kicked off by doing 600 push-ups and 240 pull-ups in 2 hours, and it went live on Facebook. Every minute five push-ups and two pull-ups were done.

Did it feel good? Absolutely not!

But was it worth the effort? Damn right it was!

Look at all the things that happened because one person decided to share his life with an orphaned woman. So whenever an idea pops into your head, trust the idea and make use of it in the real world. Thoughts, words and actions. Once thoughts start turning into action, that is when you begin to be at your best.

"Why did it happen to me?" is a question too many of us have asked ourselves whenever we face hardships.

The only sensible reply to that is, "Why not me?"

When you stop playing the victim because something happened to you and start taking ownership of your life, that is when things start happening for you. Accepting your current situation of hardship will help you get out of the pit that you fell into. That is the first step to calm your mind because it can only come up with new ideas if it stays calm. If you keep questioning everything in life and your entire life will turn into an unanswered question. You want to calm your mind and find the solution that turns your life into a bold statement. It will be a statement that will inspire many, many others around you. When you stay strong and have a sense of direction to move ahead in life, you will attract like-minded people, and positive things will come out of it. That is how the law of attraction works. You get what you are. This is why it is essential to empower yourself.

I like to keep climbing these self-made mountains. I want to keep searching. Although it seems like I am looking for something, secretly, I hope never to find the answer. Because if I ever do, then my search will come to a stop. Suddenly, life may not seem fascinating anymore.

I cannot tell you what answers await at the peak of the mountain. Life will give you the answer. This is not the answer that you find in books.

This is the answer that will make you write books.

Keep Running, Keep Banging

CONNECT WITH

Author

jibbypeterdcruz@gmail.com
On Instagram @ jibbypeterdcruz
On Facebook @ Jibby Peter Dcruz

EMMANUEL CHARITABLE TRUST

Emmanuel Charitable Trust was founded by Bro. Thomas Nadukathara on January 22 in 2005, in Thodupuzha in Kerala. The Trust is registered as a Nonprofit Social Organization working for child development across India. Emmanuel Charitable Trust closely works with the deprived communities and empowers the socially marginalized by providing them livelihood services and imparting skills leading to employment, health, and education facilities. The organization also focuses on livelihood services, child rights, human rights, young girls' education, skill development, and other community services.

Contact:

Emmanuel Charitable Trust,

Thodupuzha P.O. P.B No. 38,

Mangattukavala, Idukki district,

Kerala, India - 685584

www.emmanuelcharitabletrust.com

Account Details

Emmanuel Charitable Trust

Bank Name: Federal Bank

Branch: Thodupuzha

Account number :11210100202839

IFSC:FDRL0001121

PRETTY LIL HEARTS

Pretty Lil Hearts (PLH) is an organization that started in 2017 with a team of three teenagers. Night tuition for underprivileged school-going children was the first act of care they devoted their time to. Through the initiative of 'Aachani', 255+ homeless and Gypsy children were benefited across the state of Tamil Nadu.

It was an encounter with a granny which changed the organization's perspective. When PLH gave her sweets and new clothes, she threw them all away and demanded food. It was this incident that initiated 'Annam' - Food Drive for Homeless and Guest of Society. Today close to 75 deserving people have the satisfaction of having at least one meal a day thanks to the organization's efforts.

Through 'Aakaatu,' the transgender community was provided food carts that enabled them to earn a livelihood independently. Seven transgenders and four widows were benefited.

But it was a magical meeting with a little girl called Blessy that made the objectives of PLH crystal clear. Blessy was a 12-year-old kid fighting a losing battle with cancer. Since then, infant and pregnancy care has been the sole focus since it was shocking to find there were no key role players in that area as an organization or as an individual. It was how the mission Infant Death-Free Nation was born in June 2018.

Other services include:

Free Transportation of Pregnant women - Amradham.

Indians first free photo booth for pregnant women in a government hospital - Ahaana Gypsy and tribal pregnant women nutritional support

As of August 2021, there are 4570+ beneficiaries in all the services mentioned above.

During the first and second waves of Covid-19, free transportation services for Covid positive pregnant women were provided, through which close to 2104+ deserving pregnant women benefited.

Recognitions Received:
World Humanitarian Drive, London.

Interview on NDTV, Aaj Thank , Republic India , ANI etc

Article on Times of India, Deccan Chronicles, The Hindu, Indian Express and other national and local media.

 Let Love Rule

www.prettylilhearts.org

THE RAIN TRUST

Mission:
To empower the underprivileged society kids by bringing a strong impact through education, cleansing the untouched people on the roadside by making a better life and creating a better future for the special kids.

Our services include:

Food For Homeless:
A project that selects homeless people and provides them with a

meal. Once a medium of trust was opened up, a livelihood was created for them by making them do small-scale work. It ensures they do not return to the street.

Cycling For A Cause:
100km and 300km cycling were done by the trust members to raise funds to provide food for the homeless.

Unnakum Kalvi:
The real sense of purpose was revealed when the organization contacted the tribal village Jarugu Hills located in Salem, Tamilnadu. Due to lack of transportation, this place was hidden from its nearby town Salem. After knowing the needs of education from the village people, a free tuition center and weekly sports training activities are conducted regularly to enhance the lives of those people.

Teach the Teachers:
It was initiated to address the needs of students with special needs. Guest lectures are given to school teachers on creating a safe environment for these special kids.

Awards:
Abdul Kalam Award of Recognition (2020)

Media Acknowledgement:
The Hindu newspaper, Sun TV, Puthiya Thalaimurai TV, J News and Polimer News.

Contact	**Account Details:**
Agharam A Center for Speech and,	The Rain Trust,
Hearing	Ph. No - 9965568070
No. 49, Pitchards Road,	Bank Name: ICICI Bank,
Opp. to Commercial Tax Office,	A/c. No: 768705000021,
Hasthampatty,	IFSC : ICIC007687,
Salem – 7	Branch: Salem Hasthampatty.
Tamil Nadu, India	www.theraintrust.com